D0454193

Immigration

Other Books of Related Interest:

Opposing Viewpoints Series

Latin America

At Issue Series

Does the World Hate the U.S.?

Current Controversies Series

Illegal Immigration

"Congress shall make no law . . . abridging the freedom of speech, or of the press."

First Amendment to the U.S. Constitution

The basic foundation of our democracy is the First Amendment guarantee of freedom of expression. The Opposing Viewpoints Series is dedicated to the concept of this basic freedom and the idea that it is more important to practice it than to enshrine it.

Immigration

David M. Haugen, Susan Musser and Kacy Lovelace,
Book Editors

GREENHAVEN PRESS
A part of Gale, Cengage Learning

Detroit • New York • San Francisco • New Haven, Conn • Waterville, Maine • London

Christine Nasso, *Publisher*
Elizabeth Des Chenes, *Managing Editor*

© 2009 Greenhaven Press, a part of Gale, Cengage Learning.

Gale and Greenhaven Press are registered trademarks used herein under license.

For more information, contact:
Greenhaven Press
27500 Drake Rd.
Farmington Hills, MI 48331-3535
Or you can visit our Internet site at gale.cengage.com

For product information and technology assistance, contact us at

Gale Customer Support, 1-800-877-4253
For permission to use material from this text or product, submit all requests online at www.cengage.com/permissions

Further permissions questions can be emailed to permissionrequest@cengage.com

Articles in Greenhaven Press anthologies are often edited for length to meet page requirements. In addition, original titles of these works are changed to clearly present the main thesis and to explicitly indicate the author's opinion. Every effort is made to ensure that Greenhaven Press accurately reflects the original intent of the authors. Every effort has been made to trace the owners of copyrighted material.

LIBRARY OF CONGRESS CATALOGING-IN-PUBLICATION DATA

Immigration / David M. Haugen, Susan Musser, Kacy Lovelace, book editors.
      p. cm. -- (Opposing viewpoints)
   Includes bibliographical references and index.
   ISBN 978-0-7377-4522-1 (hardcover)
   ISBN 978-0-7377-4523-8(pbk.)
   1. United States--Emigration and immigration. 2. Immigrants--United States. 3.
Illegal aliens--United States. I. Haugen, David M., 1969- II. Musser, Susan. III.
Lovelace, Kacy.
   JV6465.I456 2009
   304.8'73--dc22
                                                                2009014562

Printed in the United States of America
  2 3 4 5 6   14 13 12 11 10

ED083

Contents

Why Consider Opposing Viewpoints?   11

Introduction   14

Chapter 1: How Does Immigration Affect the United States?

Chapter Preface   20

1. Immigration Benefits the Economy   22
   Becky Akers and Donald J. Boudreaux

2. Illegal Immigration Hurts the Economy   30
   Art Thompson

3. Immigration Harms African American Workers   36
   Frank Morris

4. Immigration Alone Does Not Harm   45
   U.S. Workers
   Rakesh Kochhar

5. Immigrants Burden Social Services   50
   Steven A. Camarota

6. Immigrants Do Not Burden Social Services   55
   Shikha Dalmia

Periodical Bibliography   60

Chapter 2: How Should the United States Contend with Its Nonnative Speakers?

Chapter Preface   62

1. English Should Be America's Official Language 64
   Kenneth Blackwell

2. Efforts to Make English America's   69
   Official Language Hide Bigotry
   Lloyd Garver

3. English Immersion Education Benefits
   Immigrant Children
   Christine Rossell
                                                      74

4. English Immersion Education Is Flawed
   Margaret Adams and Kellie M. Jones
                                                      85

Periodical Bibliography   96

Chapter 3: How Should the United States Deter Illegal Immigration?

Chapter Preface   98

1. A Border Fence Will Deter Illegal Immigration
   Duncan Hunter
                                                     100

2. A Border Fence Will Not Deter
   Illegal Immigration
   Melanie Mason
                                                     105

3. Employment Verification Will Deter
   Illegal Immigration
   Robert E. Rector
                                                     112

4. Employment Verification Will Not Deter
   Illegal Immigration
   Tom DeWeese
                                                     122

5. The United States Should Adopt
   Open Immigration
   Harry Binswanger
                                                     132

6. The United States Should Not Adopt
   Open Immigration
   Vin Suprynowicz
                                                     141

7. Lax Immigration Policies Invite Terrorism
   Mark Krikorian
                                                     147

Periodical Bibliography   162

Chapter 4: Does Immigration Threaten National Security?

Chapter Preface   164

1. The Visa Waiver Program Is a Security Threat   166
   Dan Stein

2. The Visa Waiver Program Is Not   174
   a Security Threat
   Daniel Griswold

3. Aliens Who Overstay Their Visas Are   182
   a Serious Security Threat
   Jessica M. Vaughan

4. Aliens Who Overstay Their Visas Are Not   194
   a Serious Security Threat
   Margaret D. Stock

5. Illegal Immigrants Are a Threat   203
   to National Security
   Jan C. Ting

Periodical Bibliography   213

For Further Discussion   214

Organizations to Contact   218

Bibliography of Books   225

Index   229

Why Consider Opposing Viewpoints?

> *"The only way in which a human being can make some approach to knowing the whole of a subject is by hearing what can be said about it by persons of every variety of opinion and studying all modes in which it can be looked at by every character of mind. No wise man ever acquired his wisdom in any mode but this."*
>
> *John Stuart Mill*

In our media-intensive culture it is not difficult to find differing opinions. Thousands of newspapers and magazines and dozens of radio and television talk shows resound with differing points of view. The difficulty lies in deciding which opinion to agree with and which "experts" seem the most credible. The more inundated we become with differing opinions and claims, the more essential it is to hone critical reading and thinking skills to evaluate these ideas. Opposing Viewpoints books address this problem directly by presenting stimulating debates that can be used to enhance and teach these skills. The varied opinions contained in each book examine many different aspects of a single issue. While examining these conveniently edited opposing views, readers can develop critical thinking skills such as the ability to compare and contrast authors' credibility, facts, argumentation styles, use of persuasive techniques, and other stylistic tools. In short, the Opposing Viewpoints Series is an ideal way to attain the higher-level thinking and reading skills so essential in a culture of diverse and contradictory opinions.

In addition to providing a tool for critical thinking, Opposing Viewpoints books challenge readers to question their own strongly held opinions and assumptions. Most people form their opinions on the basis of upbringing, peer pressure, and personal, cultural, or professional bias. By reading carefully balanced opposing views, readers must directly confront new ideas as well as the opinions of those with whom they disagree. This is not to simplistically argue that everyone who reads opposing views will—or should—change his or her opinion. Instead, the series enhances readers' understanding of their own views by encouraging confrontation with opposing ideas. Careful examination of others' views can lead to the readers' understanding of the logical inconsistencies in their own opinions, perspective on why they hold an opinion, and the consideration of the possibility that their opinion requires further evaluation.

Evaluating Other Opinions

To ensure that this type of examination occurs, Opposing Viewpoints books present all types of opinions. Prominent spokespeople on different sides of each issue as well as well-known professionals from many disciplines challenge the reader. An additional goal of the series is to provide a forum for other, less known, or even unpopular viewpoints. The opinion of an ordinary person who has had to make the decision to cut off life support from a terminally ill relative, for example, may be just as valuable and provide just as much insight as a medical ethicist's professional opinion. The editors have two additional purposes in including these less known views. One, the editors encourage readers to respect others' opinions—even when not enhanced by professional credibility. It is only by reading or listening to and objectively evaluating others' ideas that one can determine whether they are worthy of consideration. Two, the inclusion of such viewpoints encourages the important critical thinking skill of objectively evaluating an author's credentials and bias. This evaluation will illuminate an author's reasons for taking a particular stance on an issue and will aid in readers' evaluation of the author's ideas.

It is our hope that these books will give readers a deeper understanding of the issues debated and an appreciation of the complexity of even seemingly simple issues when good and honest people disagree. This awareness is particularly important in a democratic society such as ours in which people enter into public debate to determine the common good. Those with whom one disagrees should not be regarded as enemies but rather as people whose views deserve careful examination and may shed light on one's own.

Thomas Jefferson once said that "difference of opinion leads to inquiry, and inquiry to truth." Jefferson, a broadly educated man, argued that "if a nation expects to be ignorant and free . . . it expects what never was and never will be." As individuals and as a nation, it is imperative that we consider the opinions of others and examine them with skill and discernment. The Opposing Viewpoints Series is intended to help readers achieve this goal.

David L. Bender and Bruno Leone,
Founders

Introduction

"We're a nation of laws, and we must enforce our laws. We're also a nation of immigrants, and we must uphold that tradition, which has strengthened our country in so many ways. These are not contradictory goals. America can be a lawful society and a welcoming society at the same time."

President George W. Bush,
May 2006 Address
on Immigration Reform

"Today's immigrants seek to follow in the same tradition of immigration that has built this country. We do ourselves and them a disservice if we do not recognize the contributions of these individuals. And we fail to protect our Nation if we do not regain control over our immigration system immediately."

Senator Barack Obama,
April 2006 Statement
on Immigration Reform

The U.S. Census Bureau reports that 37.9 million immigrants resided in the United States in 2007. Of those, the Office of Immigration Statistics—a branch of the Department of Homeland Security—estimates that 11.8 million were here illegally. This latter figure shows a rise from 2000 when the number of illegal immigrants was 8.5 million.

The growing illegal population has been a concern for U.S. politicians for some time, and many have promised reform. In 2006, President George W. Bush made immigration reform the subject of one of his prime-time telecasts to the nation. In it, he claimed, "Illegal immigration puts pressure on public schools and hospitals, it strains state and local budgets, and brings crime to our communities." The President acknowledged that it would be impractical and unfair to deport the millions of illegal immigrants that are already part of the United States' communities. Bush said, "I believe that illegal immigrants who have roots in our country and want to stay should have to pay a meaningful penalty for breaking the law, to pay their taxes, to learn English, and to work in a job for a number of years." At the same time, he advocated barring the door to further illegal traffic. Therefore, he urged lawmakers to pass comprehensive legislation that would secure the nation's borders while helping those already here to assimilate into U.S. society.

In 2007, Congress debated the Secure Borders, Economic Opportunity and Immigration Reform Act of 2007 but failed to vote on the measure. This bill, which President Bush supported, would have enhanced border security by increasing the number of border patrol agents and providing funds for more vehicle barriers and other physical deterrents along the U.S.-Mexico border. More controversially, the act would have granted illegal aliens a special visa that, after eight years, could be turned into a permanent resident card if the holder agreed to pay a fine of $2000 and any back taxes owed while he or she worked in the country. The Secure Borders, Economic Opportunity and Immigration Reform Act never emerged from the Senate where, according to the *Washington Times*, "a majority of senators voted to block it, responding to millions of e-mails, phone calls and faxes from voters furious over a measure they saw as amnesty."

Although clearly a hot-button issue in 2007, the topic of illegal immigration seemed to fade from political prominence during the presidential election race in 2008. Republican candidate John McCain was a supporter of the Immigration Reform Act. When it failed, he fell back to a protectionist view that placed emphasis on securing the nation's borders first. "When we have achieved our border security goal," McCain wrote, "we must enact and implement the other parts of practical, fair and necessary immigration policy." Barack Obama the Democratic nominee supported border security but advocated the fast-tracking of illegal residents to become U.S. citizens through the special visa program. The Obama camp added that the government "must fix the dysfunctional immigration bureaucracy and increase the number of legal immigrants to keep families together and meet the demand for jobs that employers cannot fill." Despite these party-line positions, the two candidates never tackled immigration in their face-to-face debates and addressed the issue only slightly in their own campaign agendas, giving more time to the pressing issues of the flagging economy and the Iraq war.

The *Christian Science Monitor* claimed the subject of immigration reform was "too complex and highly contentious" to become a mainstay of campaign platforms on either side. Republicans feared that their general anti-amnesty stance would turn off Hispanic voters, and Democrats knew that tough talk on border security and crackdowns on undocumented workers would likewise not endear them to immigrants. Ali Noorani, the executive director of the pro-immigrant National Immigration Forum, went so far as to say that "the candidates and the media have ghettoized the immigrant community and the issue of immigration" in the election race.

The success of Barack Obama in securing the presidency in the 2008 election, however, showed that Republicans may have done more damage to their relationship with immigrant communities—especially the large population of Latinos. According to CBS News, 67 percent of Hispanics voted for Obama, while only 31 percent voted for McCain. By contrast,

George W. Bush had won 44 percent of Hispanics' votes in 2004. CBS credits the Democrats' windfall to Obama' stance on the economy and not his position on immigration reform. Still, the news service suggests that the Republicans lost Hispanic voters because Latinos expected McCain to simply carry on the policies of George W. Bush. Representative Tom Tancredo, a Republican from Colorado, disputes the charge, saying that patterns in Hispanics' voting "did not change radically in 2008" and reinforcing the notion that immigration policy did not influence the majority of Latinos to vote Democratic.

Democrats may also be losing control of their bid to bring about comprehensive immigration reform that would put illegal aliens on the path toward citizenship. In December 2008, Senator Ted Kennedy, a supporter of reform legislation, decided to focus his attention on health care instead of immigration. Kennedy had been chairman of the Senate Judiciary Subcommittee on Immigration for years and had authored a 2005 bill on immigration reform, and some people saw his shift of focus away from the issue of immigration as a sign of resignation that the Obama administration would not be able to make the issue a priority. Randel Johnson, vice president of labor, immigration, and employee benefits at the U.S. Chamber of Commerce, said that Kennedy's shift "will adversely affect immigration reform going forward. It indicates the chances of comprehensive reform happening over the next few years are slim." However, some believe that even without Kennedy's forceful hand, immigration will likely be a government priority. Washington journalist Gebe Martinez, writing on Politico.com, claims that President Obama must face the issue directly. Martinez notes, "Given that it intersects with the economy, health care, education and other key concerns, immigration is too complex a topic to ignore."

Americans must wait and see if Congress and the President can bring comprehensive immigration reform to the forefront in the opening years of the new Democratic administration. Yet even if such legislation passes, the problems and concerns associated with legal and illegal immigration will not disappear overnight. In *Opposing Viewpoints: Immigration*, a host of advocates and critics of immigration reform, as well as other policies affecting immigrants, debate these issues in chapters titled How Does Immigration Impact the United States? How Should the United States Contend with Its Nonnative Speakers? How Should the United States Deter Illegal Immigration? and Does Immigration Threaten National Security? These analysts and pundits approach immigration issues from various points on the political spectrum, but all of them recognize that the United States is a nation of immigrants and a beacon to people in other countries who wish to experience the freedoms and opportunities that are uniquely American.

OPPOSING
VIEWPOINTS®
SERIES

How Does Immigration Affect the United States?

Chapter Preface

In a Spring 2007 issue of *Americas Quarterly,* Steven A. Camarota, the director of research at the Center for Immigration Studies, asserts that the flood of immigrants into the United States negatively affects low-skilled, low-wage-earning Americans. Camarota explains that because low-paid U.S. workers typically have little education beyond high school, they are the economic rivals of poorly educated immigrants who unfortunately outnumber the native-born Americans by nearly four to one. Camarota writes, "Common sense, economic theory, and a fair reading of the research on this question indicate that allowing in so many immigrants (legal and illegal) with relatively little education reduces the wages and job prospects for Americans with little education." In Camarota's view, then, the sheer number of immigrants means that poorly educated Americans have only a one in five chance of securing the majority of low-skill jobs offered by U.S. employers.

Nancy Urban, a linguist focusing on political affairs, maintains that such an assertion inaccurately portrays the job conditions of immigrants—especially of the numerous immigrants coming from Mexico and Latin America. Urban claims that immigrants are hired more often for low-skill jobs because U.S. employers can get away with paying them less than native-born Americans would take. "Often these workers have no other choice than to work for less than legal workers earn," Urban notes, because earning these depressed wages is still a better choice than facing no employment in their homelands.

Steven Malanga, a senior fellow at the Manhattan Institute, an economic think tank, counters that allowing in so many immigrants—both illegal and legal—to take low-skill jobs is still problematic for other reasons. In Malanga's opinion, "the availability of cheap workers has led businesses to suspend investment in new technologies that would make them less labor-intensive." Thus, the large pool of low-wage-earning immigrants is allowing industry to forgo innovations that would improve the conditions for its workers. Malanga advocates that the United States learn to restrict its immigration policies and focus on attracting higher-skilled foreigners who would contribute to advancement of the economy and not languish in the host of unskilled labor.

In this chapter, various analysts—including Steven A. Camarota—debate the impact immigrants are having on the U.S. economy. Camarota insists that the tide of immigrants not only steals jobs from Americans but also burdens the taxpayers who end up funding social services for immigrant populations. Others take a different view, claiming that immigrants do not drain tax money and in fact significantly boost the United States' economic strength by providing necessary labor and adding their purchasing power to U.S. markets.

"Immigrants actually increase wages in the long run."

Immigration Benefits the Economy

Becky Akers and Donald J. Boudreaux

In the following viewpoint, Becky Akers and Donald J. Boudreaux examine the ways in which immigrant workers provide a boost to the U.S. economy by making it more efficient and productive. Akers and Boudreaux argue that this increased efficiency results in higher wages for all U.S. workers and improves the economy. Furthermore, they ground their opinion that immigrants should be allowed to contribute to the U.S. economy in the Constitutional and legal precepts that guarantee all immigrants the opportunity to pursue life, liberty, and happiness in the United States. Becky Akers is a historian and freelance writer who contributes to publications such as lewrockwell.com and counterpunch.org; Donald J. Boudreaux serves as chairman of the economics department at George Mason University.

Becky Akers and Donald J. Boudreaux, "Why Restrict Immigration at All? The Constitution and the Laws of Economics Compel Us to Welcome All Immigrants," *Christian Science Monitor*, vol. 99, June 7, 2007. Reproduced by permission of the authors.

As you read, consider the following questions:

1. What are some of the groups of people the authors identify as being banned from immigrating to the United States in past decades?

2. According to the authors' reading of Adam Smith's *Inquiry Into the Nature and Causes of the Wealth of Nations*, how do more workers increase production and prosperity?

3. Where do the authors report wages to be higher: areas like New York with many immigrants or areas like Mississippi with few immigrants?

D espite passionate disagreement, voices across the political spectrum concur on two points: They insist the federal government should do *something* about immigration, and they're sure immigrants threaten American jobs.

People assert these claims as though they're self-evident. But they aren't, as even a basic understanding of the U.S. Constitution and the principles of economics shows. And that means most of the premises about immigration are confused.

Real reform must build on the secure foundation of constitutional and economic truth—not on political talking points.

Immigration Law Is Outside Federal Government Jurisdiction

The U.S. government has been tinkering with immigration law for decades now. Surveying the wreckage—heartbroken families, an underclass of exploited workers, and ruined lives—makes it clear why the Founding Fathers refused to trust the national government with power over immigrants.

That's right: The Constitution does not authorize the federal government to control immigration. Nor does it say anything about illegal aliens. . . .

Sadly, lawmakers have repeatedly interpreted this silence as license for ill-conceived legislation. Congress began barring entry to the nation in 1875 with prostitutes and convicts. Soon, all sorts of people fell short of congressional glory: ex-convicts in 1882, along with Chinese citizens, lunatics, and idiots. Paupers, polygamists, and people suffering from infectious diseases or insanity made the list in 1891, while the illiterate were banned in 1917.

The biggest spur to antiforeigner fervor is always the same: natives fear that newcomers will swipe their jobs. Take, for example, the 1889 Supreme Court case challenging the Chinese Exclusion Act [which officially banned Chinese citizens from immigrating to the United States in 1882]. The Court upheld the exclusion because the Chinese had competed "with our artisans and mechanics, as well as our laborers in the field. . . . [Californians wanted] prompt action . . . to restrict their immigration."

Immigrants Increase Wages

It seems neither Californians nor the Court understood a fundamental principle of economics: the division of labor. Too bad they hadn't read [political philosopher and economist] Adam Smith's *Inquiry Into the Nature and Causes of the Wealth of Nations*. Published in 1776, it explains how prosperity results from more workers and better specialization.

Suppose that 10 workers produce 20 chairs per week with each worker building a complete chair. Those same workers can produce many more chairs every week if they specialize.

When one worker saws the wood, another carves it into shape, and a third fastens the pieces, the total output rises dramatically. Greater specialization leads to greater production and greater prosperity. Adding another five workers to the original 10 multiplies the benefits.

It's true that immigrants can temporarily reduce wages for Americans whose skills closely match theirs. But falling wages raise profits. And higher profits are the soil from which better wages grow.

Seeking those superior returns, investors bring more capital—more machines, expertise, stores, and new firms—while entrepreneurs learn to enhance employee output.

Specialization deepens. Workers' productivity soars, forcing employers to compete for their time by offering higher pay. Immigrants actually increase wages in the long run.

For proof, look around. The U.S. work-force has more than doubled since World War II, yet workers' real total compensation (wages plus benefits) is higher now than ever. Notice that Manhattan's employees make more money than Mississippi's. If hordes of workers depressed wages, New York City's crowds would earn far less than Mississippi's few. But paychecks in Manhattan—even for unskilled workers—trump those of workers in sparsely populated Mississippi.

Given the talk about point systems, guest-worker programs, and fenced borders, you'd think immigration endangers America's cultural and economic wealth. But just as the unhampered flow of goods and services—free trade—blesses participants, the easy flow of workers—free labor markets—also brings unprecedented prosperity.

By contrast, schemes to control immigrants hurt everyone, native or newcomer, and not just economically. Customs agents often abuse immigrants at the borders, but they also interrogate, search, and fine returning Americans.

Immigrants must produce the proper papers for bureaucrats' inspection, but so do their American employers and landlords. And let's not even think about the scary implications of the draconian Real ID Act [which was signed into law in 2005 and mandates that state-issued IDs meet federally set standards of security].

Immigrants Reduce the Cost of Goods and Services

What are the consequences of immigration for the United States? Are we economically better or worse off as a result of immigration? A misconception of some policymakers (or perhaps a position they take for rhetorical convenience) is that each immigrant who gets a job displaces one U.S.-born worker. Because the scale of the U.S. economy is not fixed, however, this extreme position is unwarranted. Immigrants are not just workers, after all, but consumers, and immigrant demand for products and services expands employment.

The story would end there if immigrants had skills in the same proportions as U.S. workers. Because immigrants are disproportionately low skilled, however, Americans benefit from immigration. Economic theory says that immigration makes other inputs into production—like skilled labor and land—relatively "scarce," and therefore raises their market value. To put it into concrete terms, if there are more low-skilled workers per acre of land, farmers can harvest more crops per acre of land, so their land is more valuable. U.S. consumers also benefit to the extent that immigrants drive down the cost of goods and services which use a lot of low-skilled labor, such as household production (maids and nannies). In a recent study, [economics professor Patricia] Cortes studied the impact of immigration on prices in 25 large U.S. metropolitan areas. She found that a 10% increase in immigration lowered the price of "low-skilled intensive" goods and services by 1%. The overall benefits to the U.S. economy are probably not trivial. . . .

Ethan Lewis, "The Impact of Immigration on American Workers and Businesses," Choices, 1ˢᵗ Quarter, 2007.

Welcoming but Not Supporting Immigrants

As technology and globalization continue shrinking the world, people and ideas move more quickly and freely. Political borders become increasingly irrelevant. But that's fine because the qualities that define Americans don't depend on geography. Rather, it's their history of liberty, pluck, ingenuity, optimism, and the pursuit of happiness. Culture is a matter of mind and spirit. Why entrust it to politicians, border guards, and green cards?

The ideal immigration policy for this smaller world would harmonize with both the Constitution and common decency. It wouldn't deny anyone the inalienable right to come and go.

This freedom perishes under current immigration edicts—and so do people. The U.S. Border Patrol estimates that almost 2,000 would-be Americans died along the U.S.-Mexican border from 1998 to 2004, whether from drowning, exposure, car accidents, or violence.

And who can forget Elian Gonzalez, the tragic Cuban refugee? This little boy watched his mother and 10 other adults in their battered boat die at sea [as they tried to flee Cuba and enter the United States illegally] largely because both U.S. and Cuban laws forbid Cubans to immigrate here. We expect such tyranny from Fidel Castro—but from America's supposedly free government?

If Congress seriously wants reform, it might begin by returning decisions on immigration to the individuals involved, in obedience to the Constitution's Ninth and 10th Amendments [which guarantee rights of the people and of states, respectively].

But Congress will need to go further. Requiring taxpayers to subsidize immigrants' healthcare, education, food, shelter, or anything else breeds resentment.

Plenty of private charities will extend a hand to newcomers, not to mention friends and families eager to help their countrymen adjust to American life.

In fact, so eager are these folks that only severe penalties discourage them: Maybe that's why the House of Representatives in 2005 passed a bill threatening to imprison for up to five years anyone who "assists, encourages, directs, or induces [an alien] to reside in or remain in the United States."

What do we do about the 12 million illegal immigrants already here? Apologizing for their poor welcome is a start. Then we can hire them, patronize their businesses, become friends. So long as we don't control them, and they don't expect our taxes to support them, goodwill should prevail on both sides.

Unconstitutional Immigration Laws

Laws labeling some people legal and others illegal aren't just divisive, they're unconstitutional. Defending America's integrity doesn't mean more rules and stronger walls; it means seeing foreigners as free agents with all the dignity and autonomy we demand for ourselves.

These people often overcome unspeakable hardship to immigrate; why add to their sorrows by making it difficult for them to become Americans? Or by forcing them to buy their citizenship? Surely, the federal coffers are bloated enough that the government need not prey on the poor and vulnerable.

Remember, too, that these folks aren't terrorists; they're here to work. And many experts argue that the safest antiterror policy is to focus scarce resources on genuine threats rather than to try to screen potential terrorists at the borders.

The federal government has controlled immigration for more than a century now. During those years, it has violated the Constitution to oppress immigrants. It has ignored economic reality by implying that immigrants depress wages and steal jobs. Both tactics pit us against each other while boosting the government's power.

Quota-wielding bureaucrats should not define the country's demographic destiny. It's time to let the free choices of millions of individuals determine America's complexion.

> *"The immigration problem has grown so big that unless it is solved, it will prove an impediment to economic recovery and an obstacle to future economic growth."*

Illegal Immigration Hurts the Economy

Art Thompson

In the viewpoint that follows, Art Thompson states that illegal immigration is one of the main causes of the economic downturn in 2008. He argues that only through more stringent immigration policies will the economy be able to recover and grow. Thompson argues that many illegal immigrants took out subprime home loans that they could not afford, which was a major factor contributing to the failure of the housing market. The author also outlines the ways in which illegal immigration hurts the economy, from contributing to violence and prison overcrowding to shrinking the American workforce. Art Thompson is the CEO of the John Birch Society, a conservative public policy organization.

Art Thompson, "Real Solutions for the Economy: Stop Illegal Immigration," *John Birch Society*, www.jbs.org, November 12, 2008. Reproduced by permission.

As you read, consider the following questions:

1. How did illegal immigration contribute to the failure of the mortgage and housing industry, according to the author?

2. What are some of the ways that the author believes illegal immigration has contributed to economic hardship in the United States in recent years?

3. The author states that immigrants from what two countries are responsible for increases in organized crime syndicates in American cities?

While it may not seem that illegal immigration has anything to do with economic solutions and recovery, there are several things which must be taken into account when discussing the full scope of what recovery means.

If in massive numbers, illegal immigration constitutes an invasion, it doesn't matter the reason for the immigration. From the Visigothic invasion of the Roman Empire, to the illegal immigration into the United States, they are state-changing events. A country must have control of its borders, who may enter, and the flow of capital into it, or the country will cease to exist.

Immigrants and the Mortgage Crisis

Subsidizing illegal immigrants' medical care, schooling, and housing is a billions of dollars per year proposition. The burdens on the hospitals have been extraordinary and the costs staggering. In California in 2004, the cost for unreimbursed health care was estimated at $1.4 billion. That's a large amount of money, but it becomes larger when the costs from other states are added to the total. Those costs then become a significant drag on the economy, but in real terms, it means less money in the pockets of American citizens. The same applies to the schools. And the lion's share of the financial burden is carried by local property owners and subsidized by federal tax monies. Much of the problem of mortgage failures [of 2008] was due to enticing illegals, who did not understand the ensuing obligations, to take out subprime home loans [loans given to individuals with a higher risk of not paying the debt, as defined by their poor or limited credit history], which failed. Subprime lenders made a special effort to attract immigrants, legal or illegal, into taking these loans, as columnist Michelle Malkin has pointed out, with ads proclaiming: "'¡Sin verificacion de ingresos! ¡Sin verificacion de documento!'—which loosely translates as, 'Income tax forms are not required, nor are immigration papers.'"

Says Malkin with regard to the economic crisis: "There's one giant paternal elephant in the room that has slipped notice: How illegal immigration, crime-enabling banks, and open-borders [George W.] Bush policies fueled the mortgage crisis."

It is interesting to note that by and large the same forces manipulating the panic of 2008 are those who welcome the massive immigration. What we are witnessing is a deliberate plan to change the United States into a socialist, controlled state. Massive immigration is part of the plan and that is why our would-be rulers have no interest in stopping it. It is important to note: the immigrants are, by and large, not the villains. They are being victimized and used by ruling elitist internationalists for ends that are not their own. The real villains are those who have used and continue to use illegal immigration as a wedge to force changes on the American people. . . .

The Widespread Negative Impact of Illegal Immigration

Another very important aspect of recovery is understanding the human toll and the resulting effect on the economy of illegal immigration. While the average illegal immigrant is a worker displaced by internationalist economic policies like NAFTA [North American Free Trade Agreement], there is a

Sanctuary Policies Protect Criminals

Some of the most violent criminals at large today are illegal aliens. Yet in cities where the crime these aliens commit is highest, the police cannot use the most obvious tool to apprehend them: their immigration status. In Los Angeles, for example, dozens of members of a ruthless Salvadoran prison gang have sneaked back into town after having been deported for such crimes as murder, assault with a deadly weapon, and drug trafficking. Police officers know who they are and know that their mere presence in the country is a felony. Yet should a cop arrest an illegal gangbanger for felonious reentry, it is he who will be treated as a criminal, for violating the LAPD's rule against enforcing immigration law.

The LAPD's ban on immigration enforcement mirrors bans in immigrant-saturated cities around the country, from New York and Chicago to San Diego, Austin, and Houston. These "sanctuary policies" [which were developed to encourage illegal immigrants to report crimes without fear of deportation due to their own status] generally prohibit city employees, including the cops, from reporting immigration violations to federal authorities.

Heather Mac Donald,
"The Illegal-Alien Crime Wave,"
City Journal, Winter 2004.

very real criminal component utilizing the dislocations caused by massive immigration to cover crimes of every variety, from drug trafficking to murder. This does not [account] for irresponsible driving habits that also take a toll of American citizens. This writer has two friends in two separate incidents that were killed by errant aliens. In both case, the aliens fled across the border to avoid vehicular manslaughter [charges]. . . .

The cost of lives is also an economic minus; those Americans who lost their lives as a result of illegal immigration would have contributed materially to the productivity of our economy, just as they would have contributed to the richness of their families and to the richness of American culture.

Our prisons overflow with inmates, a large number of whom are illegal aliens. The negative impact on the economy, both in lost wealth by our citizens through crime and additionally through the taxes to support the justice system and house criminals in prison, should be plainly seen.

Many are unaware of the crimes being committed by illegal aliens to intimidate Black Americans, forcing them to move from their neighborhoods, opening them up for illegal occupation. This is often perpetrated by vicious street gangs. This causes further stress on local economies relative to businesses, housing prices, moving costs, and mortgages. It is usually a net loss for those forced out.

Many libertarians and businessmen feel that they should be able to hire illegals since it is cheap labor, and cheap labor is a boon to the economy. But this is not true if the wages and Social Security payments end up in the illegals' homeland. It may be good for the employer, but not the economy overall.

Lastly, massive immigration leads to Balkanization [fragmentation of a region into sometimes hostile and noncooperative states] and the lack of assimilation. This is a powder keg ready to be lit by those who wish to rule. The Aztlan movement, the desire to make the American Southwest part of Mexico, among Latinos is only one example. If this powder keg is ignited, imagine what destruction and effect this will have on the economy.

A Problem That Must Be Solved

Other legal massive immigration is also taking place under the auspices of the Federal government, and it is relatively unknown to the American taxpayer. Tens of thousands of foreigners are being brought into the United States and these thousands are being subsidized by the taxpayers. The Hmong and Burmese refugees [who opposed their government and have been forced to leave their countries] are only two examples that are being settled all over the country.

We likewise are seeing crime syndicates composed of immigrants growing in major cities among the numbers of Russians and Chinese who have come into our country over the past 15 years. It is serious and [there is] a good deal of evidence that these mafia types are controlled by individuals in their mother countries.

Crime in any form takes a heavy economic toll.

This is not to say that we should build a wall around the United States and prevent any and all immigration. It is only to recognize the fact that in the U.S. today, immigration is no longer under control. As a result, immigrants and American citizens alike suffer. The immigration problem has grown so big, that unless it is solved, it will prove an impediment to economic recovery and an obstacle to future economic growth.

| "There seems to be a selective American collective memory lapse about the negative effect of mass immigration . . . upon our African American population."

Immigration Harms African American Workers

Frank Morris

Frank Morris, a board member for the Center for Immigration Studies, argues in the following viewpoint that immigration disproportionately affects African American workers. Morris contends that, throughout history, the immigrant community in the United States has taken many of the jobs that would otherwise have been filled by African Americans. He states that this has been possible because white Americans, as well as immigrants who open businesses in the United States, have historically shown a preference for immigrant labor over African American labor. Morris worries that if this problem is not addressed, African Americans will continue to suffer the ill effects of increased immigration in America. Frank Morris formerly served as the Executive Director of the Congressional Black Caucus Foundation and was Dean of Graduate Studies at Morgan State University.

Frank Morris, "American Immigration and African American Interests," *Testimony before Committee on the Judiciary*, Subcommittee on Immigration and Claims, March 11, 1999. Reproduced by permission of the author.

As you read, consider the following questions:

1. Morris states that immigration has a disproportionate effect in what states and cities?

2. What myth about immigration does the author label as fallacious, and what does he argue to be the truth?

3. According to the author, how do immigrant owners of small businesses treat African Americans in the community where their businesses operate?

Our current policies are permitting one of the greatest if not the greatest wave of immigration at a time of great economic restructuring in America when real wages for the less educated have been stagnant and have only slowly begun to rise at the end of our unusual lengthy economic expansion; when the demand for unskilled American labor is on the decline and we continue to lose jobs in manufacturing, we Americans are admitting more immigrants than all the rest of the world combined, and the great majority of those immigrants are unskilled.

Immigration is a clear example of many issues that currently have great impact upon African Americans, but many African American political leaders either ignore it or act contrary to the interests of the African American community. This was not always the case. Until the end of World War II all African American leaders of stature always opposed large scale mass American immigration. Their reasons were clear. First, American immigration policies were biased against people of color. Second, they realized that African Americans (after slavery was abolished) were more likely to benefit from an American economy which suffered from a labor shortage rather than one with a labor surplus. Third, they realized that since African Americans were always the last hired and the first fired in labor markets, Americans seemed to prefer any available labor market supply before African Americans. Most of these conditions still persist. . . . The differences of the present from the past do not justify the lack of African American attention to this issue or the lack of African American political opposition to American immigration at this scale under current American economic conditions.

Too often the true impact of our current immigration policies on African American communities is either ignored, distorted, or not considered important enough to be given great weight or consideration in this debate. My point is not to devalue the immigrant experience, but to make the often ignored points that not only did all Americans not have an immigrant experience, but more importantly, not all Americans have always benefited from an immigrant experience, especially in times of large scale mass immigration.

Historical Impact of Immigration

There seems to be a selective American collective memory lapse about the negative effect of mass immigration such as we are currently experiencing upon our African American population. The fact of life is that African Americans do not currently and have not in the past benefited from periods of mass American immigration. We do not often acknowledge that the great migration of African Americans from the rural south to the north and west did not happen until mass U.S. immigration was restricted during and after the first World War.

One of the facts of American history that is not widely discussed has been America's willingness to seem to prefer a new immigrant supply of labor when the alternative was to train and employ the more indigenous African American labor source. Booker T. Washington [African American author and community leader] in his 1895 Atlanta exposition speech pleaded with the industrialists not to look to a European labor supply but rather to the black and white labor supply in the south. Instead of providing vocational and craft training for blacks, America turned to a European immigrant pool of labor to stimulate first greater northern and western industries. African Americans were always the residual labor pool and never able to enjoy the benefits of full employment save for times of war when the preferred (white) immigrant supply was not available. African Americans were later denied (and continue to be denied) access to skilled craft guilds and labor unions. The preference and utilization of immigrant over southern black (and white) labor in the nineteenth century helped to create an economic lag time that continues to plague African Americans.... This new wave of immigration promises to continue to delay the timetable for many of our poor and less educated African Americans to enjoy the benefits of a more fair American economic justice....

Confronting Myths of Immigration

Make no mistake about it, the potential for employment is the greatest pull factor for immigration. If the supply of labor, especially unskilled labor, increases in markets where significant numbers of African Americans reside for any reason, you have either a wage depression or labor substitution effect upon African Americans who, because we have less education, work experience and small business creation rates than other Americans, are disproportionally negatively impacted in those markets. I regret to point out that it is quite possible that high rates of immigration may be permitted to continue because while almost half of African Americans work in high immigrant occupations (42%), only a little more than one in five white Americans (22%) work in high immigrant occupations.

It is important to point out that immigration is not evenly distributed across our great country, but it has disproportionate impact upon states in the South and West (Texas, California and Florida) and cities of past and present significant immigrant flow patterns (Los Angeles, Houston, Miami, Chicago, New York and Washington DC come to mind).

A fact of life is that many African American citizens are living in dire straits in most of these areas of significant immigration. I consistently confront the myth that immigrants take jobs that other Americans, such as African Americans, do not want. This is especially fallacious when we see the extent of immigrant employment in the light manufacturing, services and construction sectors.

The fact is that many African Americans, who as Americans, collectively have less access to education and higher education than other Americans, are especially anxious for job opportunities in light manufacturing, the services and especially construction. African American workers and especially young urban workers were and are being denied opportunities in construction that were given to immigrant construction workers in cities subject to high immigrant migration.

The argument is often made that the jobs that immigrants often take in our urban labor markets are jobs that others, such as African American laborers, do not want. The prototype of such jobs are often day labor positions. The assumption that African American workers do not want these positions is fallacious. According to recent data, the percent of immigrants in the labor force in the laborer and fabricator category (20%) almost equals the percentage of African Americans (22%).

Creating Social Conflict

Do not misread me. I am not posing a causal relationship. Immigrants, neither legal nor illegal, did not bring about the state of Black America. Yet the patience of African Americans wears thin when America welcomes and provides [immigrants], in this century as it did in the last, a better opportunity to achieve the American dream than it provides for African Americans.

America is the only country in the world that has mass immigration at a time of industrial restructuring of the

Perception of Immigrants Vary between African Americans and Caucasians

Blacks Have Positive Views of Immigrants ...

Immigrants from	Whites	Blacks
Latin America ...	%	%
Work very hard	78	79
Have strong family values	81	77
Significantly increase crime	34	26
Often go on welfare	37	33
Illegal immigrants ...		
Should be eligible for social services	20	43
Their children should be allowed to attend schools	67	79

But Worry About Immigrants' Impact on Jobs

Self or family member lost job to immigrant?		
Yes	14	22
No	83	71
Don't know	3	7
	100	100
Immigrants take jobs ...		
Americans don't want	65	53
Away from U.S. citizens	25	34
Both/Don't know	10	13
	100	100
Job opportunities in your community		
Plenty of jobs available	41	18
Jobs are difficult to find	52	78
Mixed/Don't know	7	4
	100	100

TAKEN FROM: Carrol Doherty, "Attitudes Toward Immigration: In Black and White," Pew Research Center Publications, April 26, 2006. www.pewresearch.org.

economy. African Americans are disproportionally hurt by this process because almost half of all immigrants head for cities that also have a large number of African American residents searching and fighting for better low-rent housing, better low-skill requirement but high-paying jobs, and better public school education for their offspring. Needless to say, as manufacturing and industrial jobs decline, the competition for the other jobs becomes more intense, and when this happens African Americans always lose for a variety of reasons. These reasons range from stereotypes about race to a preference to more vulnerable workers for whom the threat of deportation can be held over their heads.

In 1990, immigrants were 10% of the U.S. labor force and were a quarter of all workers without a high school diploma, but by 1998 immigrants were 12.2% of the workforce and 31% of immigrants did not have a high school diploma. These workers had succeeded in displacing African American workers in such areas as the construction trade, the restaurant and hospitality services and in light manufacturing in many cities. We are creating the environment for social conflict.

Immigrant Discrimination Against African Americans

As mass immigration continues, I see reports each day that spell out a continuing decline in the condition for African Americans in the country. A *Wall Street Journal* article pointed out that African Americans were the only Americans to suffer permanent job losses at our large corporations during the last recession. The worst loss of all categories was for laborers. The same pattern is still in effect for our next recession. Do not mistake this as a sign that African Americans do not want labor intensive jobs. Whenever we witness employers who have low skilled jobs available, we find many African Americans who want to work but are often not chosen. This pattern especially holds for the impressive number of small businesses started by immigrants.

It is a sad but tragic fact that most Americans, much less most immigrants, do not really identify with most African Americans as part of a great American community primarily because of our collective and often sad history together. We now have evidence that many immigrants, especially owners of Asian businesses in our large cities, actually discriminate against African Americans and especially African American youth in businesses located in Black communities. These immigrant owners actually prefer to hire illegal immigrants, especially Hispanic immigrants, over African Americans. They readily accept the negative stereotypes of African Americans extensively portrayed in the movies and on videos. This point is critical because immigrant-owned businesses account for one-quarter of all low wage jobs and one-third of the traditional entry jobs in both New York and Los Angeles. This tragedy is compounded because Black immigrants from the West Indies even discriminate against American blacks. These negative stereotypes are accepted by immigrants in spite of the fact that there are an average of 14 African American job applicants for every Harlem minimum wage job opening according to a study done by a Columbia University anthropologist. . . .

African American Workers Must Be Protected

I am consistently concerned with our deteriorating sense of an American community where we should have a greater responsibility to other Americans before we give priority to non-American citizens. We need to help protect American workers, especially low-skilled African American workers, from job displacement and [the] eventual job wage depressing effect of workers who should not be competing in the American workplace. I note, with regret, the fact that many will identify and have great sympathy for the overall plight of immigrant workers but be callous toward the fate of other Americans who have suffered from years and generations of unfair treatment. During many of these years and generations of unfair and discriminatory treatment, from other Americans to African Americans, immigrant Americans were able to benefit from employment opportunities which in the past were denied to African Americans. How unfair it is that this pattern—still strongly influenced by high immigration levels—continues to negatively affect African American workers.

Just as immigration policy was and has been a contributing factor to the limited employment opportunities for African Americans in the last century and for at least three decades of this century, it is time that the labor market effects, especially labor market effects of immigration on African Americans and other low-income workers, be addressed as a top priority. Our sense of common purpose and the brother- and sisterhood of our shared American experience should permit us to do no less. We must begin to address the gaps in our immigration policies that compound the disadvantages of our people of color at a time when the economic indicators for low income, low skilled African Americans is dismal. If we are not going to address this issue, then who will?

| *"Isolating one factor—even a big one like immigration—to explain gains or losses by US-born workers just doesn't work."*

Immigration Alone Does Not Harm U.S. Workers

Rakesh Kochhar

In the following viewpoint, Rakesh Kochhar, associate director for research at the Pew Hispanic Center, reports the findings of a recent Pew study analyzing the impact of immigrants on the U.S. workforce. Based on the findings, Kochhar argues that immigration alone cannot be singled out as a cause of job loss in the United States. He states that employment levels do not vary based on the number of immigrants in a particular state. Further, he notes that some states with a large immigrant workforce have lower levels of unemployment for Americans than do states with small immigrant workforces, leading him to assert that other factors must be considered in order to explain nationwide U.S. employment levels.

Rakesh Kochhar, "Does Immigration Hurt U.S. Workers? No Simple Answers to the Question of Why Employment Prospects Vary Across the United States," *Guardian* (UK), August 16, 2006. Copyright © 2006 Guardian Newspapers Limited. Reproduced by permission of Guardian News Service, LTD.

As you read, consider the following questions:

1. Kochhar states that the U.S. economy produces how many jobs?
2. According the Kochhar, by how much did the population of foreign-born workers increase from 1990 to 2000?
3. What are the differences in immigrant workforces between Arkansas and Nevada, and in which state was the employment rate higher for U.S.-born workers?

A debate over economic impact lies at the root of the current immigration policy impasse: does the influx from abroad help or hurt US-born workers? Both the politicians and the economists have fought themselves to an uneasy draw, and much of the public is left looking for answers.

The simple answer, however, is that there are no simple answers.

A Vast Economy

In an economy so vast that it produces jobs for 144 million people, many forces are at work all the time. Isolating one factor—even a big one like immigration—to explain gains or losses by US-born workers just doesn't work. There are many scenarios but no single, simple tale that could tip the policy debate in one direction or another.

In the United States, the population of foreign-born workers aged 16 and older increased by more than 60% between 1990 and 2000—from 17.5 million to 28 million. In several states, the foreign-born population more than doubled. In a recent report the Pew Hispanic Center examined whether there was a relationship between this migration and the employment outcomes for US-born workers.

US-born workers did well in some states where the foreign-born population rose rapidly, as well as in other states where growth was below average. They did poorly in places that drew immigrants at a fast rate, but they also did poorly in places that drew few immigrants. Nothing has emerged to conclude that increased immigration helped or hurt the employment prospects for native workers.

State-to-State Differences

For those playing the immigration numbers game, the study did point to possible winners and losers. In 2000, 15% of US-born workers lived in states where the rapid influx of foreign-born workers could possibly be seen as having a negative impact. About one quarter lived in states where the rise in the foreign-born population appears to have had no effect on their employment outcomes. The remaining 60% lived in states where the growth of the foreign-born population was below average, but these US-born workers did not consistently encounter favourable employment outcomes.

What made a state a potential winner or a loser? It is very difficult to pin it on immigration. Consider the tale of two states, Nevada and Arkansas. Both are of similar size—Nevada had a workforce of 1.5 million, and Arkansas 2 million. But in 2000, Nevada was booming—with an employment rate for US-born workers that was 7 percentage points higher than in Arkansas, which lagged behind the national average.

So what was happening with immigration? In both states, migrant workers tripled between 1990 and 2000. By the end of the decade, Arkansas had 63,000 immigrants, just 3% of the workforce, while Nevada had 300,000, approximately 20% of the workforce. In other words, US-born workers fared better in the state with a much larger immigrant workforce.

If it was not the pace of immigration or the number of immigrants, then what determined whether a state won or lost? Many other factors need to be considered. Nevada, for example, has been an economic trendsetter for the rest of the country, Arkansas less so.

Roots of the Anti-Immigration Movement

Nationally, the chief ideologues of the anti-immigration movement usually give precedence to cultural arguments over economic ones.... But their advocacy doesn't entirely explain what happened [to raise the anti-immigration movement to national prominence].

To understand that, you have examine the movement's historical antecedents—a strain of political protest that begins in the late Jacksonian era with the Know-Nothings [a mid-nineteenth century nativist political movement] and continues through the Populists [a political party advocating policies that benefit common people] of the nineteenth and twentieth centuries to today's anti-immigration movement. It is based on the displacement—sometimes with cause, sometimes without—of deep-seated social and economic anxieties onto an "out-group," and it is voiced most often by the "intermediate strata," the social and economic classes most threatened by the development of capitalism. In the nineteenth century, the intermediate strata comprised urban artisans and small farmers; in the twentieth century, small businessmen, farmers, and craft workers undermined by industrialization; and, more recently, workers who lack adequate technical training or whose jobs are being sent overseas. These workers have seen themselves as "producers" victimized by "parasites"—by Wall Street and big business from above and by an underclass of African Americans and immigrants from below.

John B. Judis, "Phantom Menace,"
New Republic, *February 13, 2008.*

Immigration Alone Not a Significant Indicator

Our study did not try to explain how or why economic growth varies from one part of the country to another. But our numbers do clarify one point: immigration alone does not explain starkly different outcomes for US-born workers. As the country continues to debate immigration policy, measures of economic impact are not likely to resolve the argument one way or another.

"Immigrant use of social services might not be a problem if they generally paid more in taxes than native-born Americans."

Immigrants Burden Social Services

Steven A. Camarota

Steven A. Camarota argues in the following viewpoint that immigrants, both legal and illegal, to the United States account for a disproportionate percentage of social services use in the country. Camarota analyzes data from the U.S. Census Bureau and concludes that immigration is at its highest level in centuries and that because immigrants generally have lower education levels than native-born Americans, they are more likely to exploit the social services available to them. He maintains that this creates a burden on these social services programs because immigrants pay significantly less in taxes than native-born Americans. Steven A. Camarota is the director of research at the Center for Immigration Studies.

As you read, consider the following questions:

1. According to data from the Census Bureau, how many immigrants were living in the United States in 2007?

Steven A. Camarota, "Immigration, Both Legal and Illegal, Puts Huge Strain on the Country," *North County Times*, December 15, 2007. Reproduced by permission.

2. The author states that immigrants account for what percentage of uninsured people in California?

3. Camarota states that education and economic success are related in what two ways?

The debate over immigration has become one of America's most heated. In a new report published by the Center for Immigration Studies, we provide a detailed picture of the nation's immigrant population. Our conclusions will probably not surprise most Californians: First, legal and illegal immigration is at record levels. Second, immigrants are generally hardworking, yet they create enormous strains on social services. Why? Put simply, many are uneducated.

An Unsustainable Rate of Immigration

Looking first at the raw numbers, the Census Bureau data we analyzed showed that the nation's immigrant population (legal and illegal) reached nearly 38 million in March of [2007]. This is the highest number in the nation's history. No nation has ever attempted to incorporate 38 million newcomers into its society. As a share of the population, one in eight U.S. residents is now an immigrant (legal and illegal), the highest level in 80 years. About one-third of immigrants are illegal aliens. Moreover, 1.5 million new immigrants (legal and illegal) continue to arrive each year.

We found that immigration has a very large effect on the low-skilled labor market. Immigrants comprise between one-fourth and one-third of workers in cleaning, construction and food service occupations. Roughly half of these immigrant workers are estimated to be illegal immigrants. In contrast, just 9 percent of journalists and 6 percent of lawyers are immigrants, and almost none are illegal immigrants. This partly explains why the argument that "immigrants only do jobs Americans don't want" is widely accepted in the media and among elites in general. But the fact is, the overwhelming majority of low-wage jobs are done by less-educated native-born Americans, not immigrants.

The Impact of Education

Unemployment and non-work has grown significantly among less-educated Americans. In 2007 there were more than 22 million adult natives (18 to 64 years of age) with no education beyond high school either unemployed or not in the labor market. Wages and benefits for such workers have also generally stagnated or declined in recent years. Most Americans do not face significant job competition from immigrants, but those who do are generally the poorest and most vulnerable.

The low-education level of many immigrants not only means that they compete with less-educated natives, it is the primary reason so many immigrants live in or near poverty, lack health insurance and use the welfare system. This is true even though a larger share of immigrant households compared to native households have at least one worker. If this problem was put on a bumper sticker it would read: "There's a high cost to cheap labor."

In California, immigrants and their young children comprise nearly 60 percent of the uninsured. Illegals alone are 27 percent. The latest data also show that almost half of those in the state's public schools are either immigrants or the child of an immigrant. We also found that 39 percent of immigrant-headed households in the state used at least one major welfare program, twice the rate for native households.

Because 38 percent of adult immigrants in California have not completed high school, six times the rate for natives, even immigrants who work full time often end up poor, lacking health insurance and accessing social services. Our welfare system, particularly food assistance, and Medicaid/Medi-Cal are geared to help low-income workers with children, which describes a very large share of immigrants.

Illegal Immigration Costs Schools

With states straining under gaping budget shortfalls, public schools throughout the country are facing some of the most significant decreases in state education funding in decades. . . .

While these massive budget deficits cannot be attributed to any single source, the enormous impact of large-scale illegal immigration cannot be ignored. *The total K-12 school expenditure for illegal immigrants costs the states nearly $12 billion annually, and when the children born here to illegal aliens are added, the costs more than double to $28.6 billion.*

This enormous expenditure of the taxpayers' hard-earned contributions does not, however, represent the total costs. Special programs for non-English speakers are an additional fiscal burden as well as a hindrance to the overall learning environment. A recent study found that dual language programs represent an additional expense of $290 to $879 per pupil depending on the size of the class. In addition, because these children of illegal aliens come from families that are most often living in poverty, there is also a major expenditure for them on supplemental feeding programs in the schools.

Jack Martin,
"Breaking the Piggy Bank: How Illegal Immigration
Is Sending School into the Red," FAIR: Federation for American
Immigration Reform, updated June 2005. www.fairus.org.

We can see just how important education is to economic success in two different ways. First, we found that immigrants with a college degree have incomes and use of social services similar to [that of] natives. Second, when we look at legal immigrants who have very little education we found that their rates of poverty and welfare use are as high or higher than [that of] illegal immigrants. For example, we found that 56 percent of households headed by a legal immigrant who lacked a high school diploma used at least one major welfare program, triple the rate for natives. This is important because an estimated 57 percent of illegal immigrants have not completed high school. Therefore, legalization would not solve the problem of low income and heavy use of social services.

Immigrants Do Not Pay Enough Taxes

Immigrant use of social services might not be a problem if they generally paid more in taxes than native-born Americans. But the median income of immigrant households is 21 percent lower in California than that of native households, and immigrant households are 36 percent larger on average. The household is the primary unit by which taxes are assessed and services paid. This means immigrants will tend to pay less in taxes than natives and tend to use more in services. This is not the same as saying immigrants do not pay taxes. In fact, even illegal immigrants pay some taxes. However, it does mean they will be a fiscal drain.

If we want to avoid these problems we are going to have to reduce the number of legal immigrants allowed in who have relatively little education. We are also going to have to enforce the law and cause illegal immigrants to go home. Of course, the immigrants themselves clearly benefit by coming to America. And this could be used to justify continuing current policy. But the latest data show that less-educated American workers, public schools, health care providers and taxpayers will feel the effects if we continue down our present path.

> *"Immigrants aren't flocking to the United States to mooch off the government."*

Immigrants Do Not Burden Social Services

Shikha Dalmia

In the viewpoint that follows, Shikha Dalmia argues that illegal immigrants do not place any drain on social services in the United States because they are often paying for services that they cannot even access, resulting in additional funds for these programs. Dalmia states that because illegal immigrants do not have valid social security numbers, they will never be able to receive the benefits of Social Security and Medicare, two programs that they currently help to fund with taxes that are automatically withheld from their paychecks. Additionally, she notes that they contribute money to state funded programs and facilities with the sales taxes they pay on all goods purchased at their local stores. Shikha Dalmia works as a senior analyst at the Reason Foundation, a think tank that promotes free market economics.

Shikha Dalmia, "Illegal Immigrants Are Paying a Lot More Taxes Than You Think: Eight Million Illegals Pay Social Security, Medicare, and Income Taxes," *Knight Ridder/Tribune News Services*, May 1, 2006. Reproduced by permission.

As you read, consider the following questions:

1. What programs does the author identify as being unavailable for illegal immigrants following passage of the 1996 welfare reform bill?
2. According to the author, how many illegal immigrants are there, and how many of them file personal income taxes?
3. The author states that illegal immigrants help to fund what programs with the state sales taxes they pay?

Denying public services to people who pay their taxes is an affront to America's bedrock belief in fairness. But many "pull-up-the-drawbridge" politicians want to do just that when it comes to illegal immigrants.

The fact that illegal immigrants pay taxes at all will come as news to many Americans. A stunning two-thirds of illegal immigrants pay Medicare, Social Security and personal income taxes. Yet, nativists like Congressman Tom Tancredo, R-Colo., have popularized the notion that illegal aliens are a colossal drain on the nation's hospitals, schools and welfare programs—consuming services that they don't pay for.

Immigrants Are Ineligible for Many Social Services

In reality, the 1996 welfare reform bill disqualified illegal immigrants from nearly all means-tested government programs, including food stamps, housing assistance, Medicaid and Medicare-funded hospitalization. The only services that illegals can still get are emergency medical care and K-12 education.

Nevertheless, Tancredo and his ilk pushed a bill through the House criminalizing all aid to illegal aliens—even private acts of charity by priests, nurses and social workers. Potentially, any [volunteer at a] soup kitchen that offers so much as a free lunch to an illegal could face up to five years in prison and seizure of assets.

The Senate bill that recently collapsed would have tempered these draconian measures against private aid. But no one—Democrat or Republican—seems to oppose the idea of withholding public services. Earlier this year, Congress passed a law that requires everyone who gets Medicaid—the government-funded health care program for the poor—to offer proof of U.S. citizenship so we can avoid "theft of these benefits by illegal aliens," as Rep. Charlie Norwood, R-Ga., puts it.

Immigrants Pay for Services They Do Not Use

But, immigrants aren't flocking to the United States to mooch off the government. According to a study by the Urban Institute, the 1996 welfare reform effort dramatically reduced the use of welfare by undocumented immigrant households, exactly as intended. And another vital thing happened in 1996: the Internal Revenue Service [IRS] began issuing identification numbers to enable illegal immigrants who don't have Social Security numbers to file taxes.

One might have imagined that those fearing deportation or confronting the prospect of paying for their safety net through their own meager wages would take a pass on the IRS's scheme. Not so. Close to 8 million of the 12 million or so illegal aliens in the country today file personal income taxes using these numbers, contributing billions to federal coffers. No doubt they hope that this will one day help them acquire legal status—a plaintive expression of their desire to play by the rules and come out of the shadows.

What's more, aliens who are not self-employed have Social Security and Medicare taxes automatically withheld from their paychecks. Since undocumented workers have only fake num-

Undocumented Immigrants Should Have Access to Healthcare

Many immigrants do not receive needed healthcare because they fear deportation. Denying healthcare to any segment of the population can lead to more extreme ailments that become more expensive to treat. . . .

Reality dictates that millions of undocumented immigrants plan to remain in the United States. Denying them healthcare services will lead to increased instances of infectious, yet treatable, diseases. The state legislatures of Georgia and Oklahoma nonetheless are trying to bar undocumented immigrants from receiving any medical care, including emergency room services. This overlooks the fact that most undocumented immigrants in the U.S. are younger workers. Since younger people tend to use less healthcare than the elderly, healthcare cost estimates for undocumented aliens tend to be exaggerated.

The denial of healthcare is not only bad policy, it is unrealistic, cruel, and violates medical ethics. Should an undocumented worker involved in an accident be denied healthcare and left in front of a hospital to die? Most physicians have ignored the laws and treated patients regardless of their immigration status. America has the moral obligation to care for those who reside here. Americans pride themselves on providing a moral compass for the rest of the world. They believe that every human life is precious and important. Denying any individual healthcare based on citizenship contradicts that belief.

Melissa Marietta,
"Undocumented Immigrants Should Receive Social Services,"
International Social Science Review, *Spring/Summer 2006.*

bers, they'll never be able to collect the benefits these taxes are meant to pay for. Last year [2005], the revenues from these fake numbers—that the Social Security administration stashes in the "earnings suspense file"—added up to 10 percent of the Social Security surplus. The file is growing, on average, by more than $50 billion a year.

Beyond federal taxes, all illegals automatically pay state sales taxes that contribute toward the upkeep of public facilities such as roads that they use, and property taxes through their rent that contribute toward the schooling of their children. The non-partisan National Research Council found that when the taxes paid by the children of low-skilled immigrant families—most of whom are illegal—are factored in, they contribute on average $80,000 more to federal coffers than they consume.

Finding an Equitable Solution for All

Yes, many illegal migrants impose a strain on border communities on whose doorstep they first arrive, broke and unemployed. To solve this problem equitably, these communities ought to receive the surplus taxes that federal government collects from immigrants. But the real reason border communities are strained is the lack of a guest worker program. Such a program would match willing workers with willing employers in advance so that they wouldn't be stuck for long periods where they disembark while searching for jobs.

The cost of undocumented aliens is an issue that immigrant bashers have created to whip up indignation against people they don't want here in the first place.... Politicians ought to set the record straight: Illegals are not milking the government. If anything, it is the other way around.

Periodical Bibliography

The following articles have been selected to supplement the diverse views presented in this chapter.

Daniel Altman	"Shattering Stereotypes about Immigrant Workers," *New York Times*, June 3, 2007.
William Armstrong	"Illegal Immigration," *New York Amsterdam News*, May 24, 2007.
James G. Forsyth	"Most Valuable Migrants," *Foreign Policy*, January-February 2007.
Moira Herbst	"High Drama Over Highly Skilled Workers," *Business Week* Online, September 12, 2007. www.businessweek.com.
Joyce Jones	"Immigrants vs. Blacks," *Black Enterprise*, June 2008.
Anna Quindlen	"Newcomers by Numbers," *Newsweek*, August 27, 2007.
Joel Millman	"As U.S. Debates Guest Workers, They Are Here Now," *Wall Street Journal*, September 18, 2006.
Lakeisha Porter	"Illegal Immigrants Should Not Receive Social Services," *International Social Science Review*, 2006.
Jason L. Riley	"Immigrant Scapegoats," *Wall Street Journal*, April 24, 2008.
Luis J. Rodriguez	"Blinded by the Border," *Progressive*, September 2008.
Andrea Batista Schlesinger	"Pro-Immigrant Populism," *Nation*, March 5, 2007.

OPPOSING
VIEWPOINTS®
SERIES

CHAPTER 2

How Should the United States Contend with Its Nonnative Speakers?

Chapter Preface

In mid-2008 U.S. Representative Dean Heller, a Republican from Nevada, introduced a bill into Congress to repeal a provision of the Voting Rights Act concerning bilingual ballots. This 1975 amendment to the act requires cities and counties to print voting ballots in multiple languages when more than 10,000 voters (or more than 5 percent of eligible voters) possess limited English skills. Heller explains this mandate is not funded by the federal government and therefore forces communities to cover the cost. It is one of many times, in Heller's view, that "the federal government encourages people not to learn the language." Heller believes that ending such initiatives will compel immigrants to assimilate into American culture and "bring linguistic unity to our election system." Walter B. Jones, a Republican Representative from North Carolina, is one of roughly 40 colleagues that support Heller's American Elections Act. Claiming that the majority of Americans agree that federal ballots should be printed only in English, Jones reiterates, "Multi-lingual ballots not only divide American voters by language and cause needless confusion at the polls, they impose an unnecessary financial burden on state and local governments."

Heller's detractors have a different view. The *Las Vegas Sun* ran its own editorial in May 2008 attacking Heller's bill as going "against great national progress in ending discrimination at polling sites." The paper reminds its readers that most voting acts were created to enable greater political participation, not abridge it. The editorial opines, "We believe that learning to speak, read and write English is important for all immigrants, and most are eventually successful. But why go to great lengths to make it difficult for or to disenfranchise those citizens whose circumstances have so far prevented them from fully gaining these skills?"

Heller's bill also does not have history on its side. All similar English-only ballot measures have been defeated in Congress—the most recent went down in 2006. Whether such a bill will be successful this time around is uncertain, but past attempts have failed chiefly because congressional opponents have cast them as discriminatory and anti–voter rights. In this chapter, four authors discuss other government and local programs that test the status of nonnative speakers in U.S. society. Some authors attest that permitting the inclusion of languages other than English in the public forum divides America and keeps ethnic minorities from feeling a part of national unity. Others contend that America is a mongrel country enriched by the infusion of tongues and dialects, revealing that the nation's strength is summed up in the motto *e pluribus unum*—"out of many, one."

| *"If you care about a child in America today, then you want that child to be able to speak English."*

English Should Be America's Official Language

Kenneth Blackwell

Kenneth Blackwell is a senior fellow at the Family Research Council, a Christian pro-family group, and at the Buckeye Institute, a free-market policy organization. Blackwell asserts in the following viewpoint that political parties should support making English the official language of the United States. In Blackwell's view, English is the language of American business and government, and people who want an opportunity to participate in either will need to master English.

As you read, consider the following questions:

1. As Blackwell relates, what percentage of Americans favor making English the official language of the United States?
2. According to Blackwell, who opposes making English the official language?

3. What economic benefits can an individual attain if he or she speaks English, in Blackwell's view?

One of the most unreported stories of the past month is Democrats in Congress refusing to protect the Salvation Army and other similar organizations from lawsuits for requiring their employees to be able to speak English on the job. This policy issue is also important politically, and Republicans will benefit politically by doing the right thing.

[Opinion columnist] John Fund's recent *Wall Street Journal* article reveals this absurd situation. Lawsuits have been brought by individuals and the Equal Employment Opportunity Commission [EEOC] against employers like the Salvation Army for requiring their employees to learn English within one year. The Salvation Army is only requiring English in performing work duties, not what language workers use in the break room, and gives them a full 12 months to learn the language. Yet the EEOC and certain groups are suing.

So Senator [Lamar] Alexander [of Tennessee] put an amendment into an appropriations bill to shield employers from these ridiculous lawsuits. The amendment passed both the House and the Senate. But the Democrats of the House Hispanic Caucus, led by Rep. Joe Baca [of California], told Speaker [Nancy] Pelosi [of California] that she needed to stop this, and she readily complied by promising to strike the language in conference, holding up the bill.

The problem is that this bill includes all the money for the Justice Department and the FBI. Critical national security, terrorist prevention, and law enforcement dollars are in that bill, and Mrs. Pelosi is caving to pressure from radical liberal groups, and in the process selling out what's best for immigrants.

The Majority of Americans Support English

I say radical liberal groups because the vast majority of Americans disagree with them. Over 80% of Americans think English should be the official language of government, almost 90% think it's very important for immigrants to be able to speak English, and over 75% believe that employers have the right to require employees to speak English while on the job.

The only ones who don't think English should be the official language are liberal activists trying to recast America in their image. Those activists also form a large part of the Democratic base, and would be unforgiving of a Democratic presidential candidate who refuses to promise amnesty, driver licenses, and free health care to illegal immigrants. Americans should disagree with this radical agenda. The simple fact is English is the commercial language of America. We speak it in business, in school, and in the press. In a workplace, it's important for safety, morale, and customer relations for everyone to be able to speak a common language.

Being fluent in English is essential if you want to succeed in America. If you're bilingual, that's even better, but a top priority for success is being able to speak English in the workplace and in the public square. Someone who can speak English can compete for better jobs, with better pay. Someone who can speak English improves their chances to have a better future for themselves and their children.

The Key to a Better Future

This is not just a Hispanic issue, or even an immigrant issue. I grew up in the inner city of Cincinnati, became mayor of this fine city, and served as the U.S. Ambassador to the United Nations Human Rights Commission. One of the greatest keys I have found to success for a young ethnic and racial minority in America today is the ability to speak, read, and write English clearly and persuasively. Anyone with good English skills can get better jobs and opportunities, and enjoy a much better life.

If you care about a child in America today, then you want that child to be able to speak English. Regardless of color or

The Costs of a Multilingual Nation

We need only look to Canada to see the problems a multilingual society can bring. America's northern neighbor faces a severe constitutional crisis over the issue of language. In 1995, the predominately French-speaking province of Quebec came within a few thousand votes of seceding from Canada. The secessionist Parti Québécois ruled the province until this year [2003]. The national government must cater to Quebec to preserve order and maintain a cohesive government. This has spurred secessionist movements in English-speaking western Canada on the grounds that the Canadian government favors French speakers.

Of course, battles over language rage across the globe, but since Canada is so similar, it offers the most instructive warning for the United States. While the policy of official multilingualism has led to disunity, resentment, and near-secession, it is also very costly. Canada's dual-language requirement costs approximately $260 million each year. Canada has one-tenth the population of the United States and spent that amount accommodating only two languages. A similar language policy would cost the United States much more than $4 billion annually, as we have a greater population and many more languages to accommodate.

Mauro E. Mujica,
"Why the U.S. Needs an Official Language,"
World and I, *December 1, 2003.*

culture, a child who knows how to communicate in English improves his or her chances for success exponentially. And part of getting children to be able to speak English is helping their parents to achieve a basic proficiency in the language by establishing some common sense requirements.

This is an issue the press needs to cover. There should be more articles and interviews on this issue. Yet John Fund's article is one of the only articles out there.

An Issue That Needs to Be Addressed

CNN [Cable News Network] should be posing this kind of question to candidates during debates, instead of ambushing Republicans with Clinton campaign plants to emphasize the issues that liberal CNN producers consider more important.

But the reason CNN doesn't talk about this is the reason conservatives should talk about it. Good policy is good politics. This is a perfect example of an issue where Republicans doing the right thing will help them in the polls. Republicans can unite the country by emphasizing English education, and holding the line on this legislation.

I'd like to see [2008 Democratic presidential candidates] Hillary Clinton and Barack Obama have to take a stand on this amendment.

An old adage says, "Give a man a fish and he'll eat for a day. Teach a man to fish and he'll eat for a lifetime." Give a person special coddling treatment in his native language, and he'll get through the day. Teach an immigrant, or anyone in this country, how to master the English language, and he can soar on eagle wings to capture the fullest measure of the American dream.

That is one thing all of us should support.

> "The English-onlies seem to want one uniform language that all Americans can understand. That's not how English was ever spoken in the United States."

Efforts to Make English America's Official Language Hide Bigotry

Lloyd Garver

In the following viewpoint, Lloyd Garver, a television writer and columnist for SportsLine.com, questions the assumptions behind those who believe English should be America's official language. As Garver notes, America was founded by immigrants who were non-English speakers, and American English has been enriched by the linguistic contributions of these immigrant groups. In Garver's view, those who advocate that all immigrants be compelled to speak English hide a prejudice against foreigners.

As you read, consider the following questions:

1. What do English-only advocates equate "old" immigrants with, according to Garver?

Lloyd Garver, "Must Everyone Speak English?" CBSNews.com, November 2, 2005. Reproduced by permission.

2. As Garver writes, why do some English-only supporters dislike the tendency of some "new" immigrants to gather in ethnic communities?

3. How could "one get carried away" with the enforcement of proper English, in Garver's opinion?

About half the states have passed laws that make English the official language of their state. Why is there a need for these laws? Isn't English already the language of the United States? Yes and no. What English-only advocates are bothered by are things like bilingual education, election information and ballots being in languages in addition to English, etc. The attitude is, "my ancestors had to learn English to get along in this country, why shouldn't the new immigrants have to do the same thing?" At first glance, it doesn't seem to be very controversial, does it? So, let's take a few more glances at it.

Not everybody learns English immediately when they come to this country. Some of us had ancestors who could barely speak English their whole lives. Many of these "old" immigrants—the ones from Europe that the English-only people seem to consider the "good" immigrants—lived in neighborhoods with other people from their homelands. That made it natural for many of them to speak the language from the old country at home. This is one thing some English-only advocates say they don't like about the "new" immigrants. They see them as cliquish people unwilling to assimilate.

Hiding a Sinister Attitude

One troublesome aspect of this movement is that while many people simply and sincerely believe that English should be the only language used in public schools and public documents, there is a more sinister attitude among some other people. Some people just hate people from foreign lands. I saw a bumper sticker on a car yesterday that read, "Speak English or Die."

States with Official English Laws

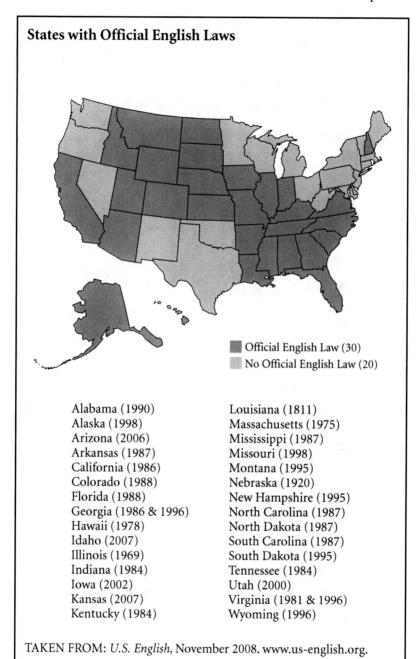

Official English Law (30)
No Official English Law (20)

Alabama (1990)
Alaska (1998)
Arizona (2006)
Arkansas (1987)
California (1986)
Colorado (1988)
Florida (1988)
Georgia (1986 & 1996)
Hawaii (1978)
Idaho (2007)
Illinois (1969)
Indiana (1984)
Iowa (2002)
Kansas (2007)
Kentucky (1984)

Louisiana (1811)
Massachusetts (1975)
Mississippi (1987)
Missouri (1998)
Montana (1995)
Nebraska (1920)
New Hampshire (1995)
North Carolina (1987)
North Dakota (1987)
South Carolina (1987)
South Dakota (1995)
Tennessee (1984)
Utah (2000)
Virginia (1981 & 1996)
Wyoming (1996)

TAKEN FROM: *U.S. English*, November 2008. www.us-english.org.

Believe it or not, I'm not the expert on heavy metal music that you may have thought I was. So, I had to go to the Internet to learn that "Speak English or Die" is the name of a song recorded by the group with the pleasant name, "Stormtroopers of Death." The chorus of the little ditty goes like this:

"You always make us wait

You're the ones we hate

You can't communicate

Speak English or die."

They also have a verse that says,

"You come into this country

You can't get real jobs

Boats and boats and boats of you

Go home, you F&*%#ing slobs."

Obviously, I have no way of measuring how many of the pro–English-only people have these prejudiced views. But just the fact that there are some is disturbing enough. These words are certainly a far cry from the inscription on the Statue of Liberty.

Many people claim that the main reason they're for this is to save money by doing away with public documents in non-English. But is that just an excuse for some bigoted people who hate "foreigners?" Are they the same people who get upset no matter where they travel in the world because the people they meet can't speak English?

A Slippery Slope

One could get carried away with this "must speak proper English" thing. For one thing, if that were a requirement for public service, George [W.] Bush could not be our president.

The English-onlies seem to want one uniform language that all Americans can understand. That's not how English was ever spoken in the United States. If a person from one part of the country has trouble understanding a person from another region, should we outlaw regional slang and accents, too?

When President Bush pronounces "nuclear" properly, maybe I'll consider getting on board. When I stop hearing good American-born citizens say things like, "That's between you and I" (instead of "between you and me"), when I stop reading the non-word "alright," when I stop hearing people tell me that something was "funner" than something else, maybe then I'll think it's time we challenged immigrants to speak as well as native-born Americans. But until we can set a better example, it's hard to be upset about new arrivals who don't speak properly.

One thing the English-onlyites seem to forget is that America has always been a melting pot. There are examples of Spanish, French, Yiddish, and German words that have been absorbed by English and are now used by Americans every day. It makes for a richer language and culture. Is there any reason to think that in the future when we start to adopt some of the language of the "new" immigrants, that English will be any less enriched?

I know some people may say that my attitude "literally" made them explode, but unless they actually blew up, they, too, should learn better English before they criticize others.

> *"My analyses show that after controlling for student and school characteristics, the average score increased by six points in reading and by three points in mathematics in schools that eliminated bilingual education."*

English Immersion Education Benefits Immigrant Children

Christine Rossell

In the following viewpoint, Christine Rossell, a professor of political science at Boston University, asserts that teaching immigrant children in English immersion classrooms is more beneficial to the students than using bilingual education. Rossell maintains that English language learners who are grouped into separate classes that are taught only in English tend to perform better when tested than do those students assigned to bilingual classrooms. She even attests that mainstreaming immigrant children into classes with native English students is preferable to bilingual education.

Christine Rossell, "Teaching English Through English," *Educational Leadership*, vol. 62, December–January 2004–2005, pp. 32–36. Copyright © 2004 by ASCD. Used with permission. Learn more about ASCD at www.ascd.org.

As you read, consider the following questions:

1. Of the six English education approaches that Rossell lists, which three does she believe are the least effective for immigrant children?

2. Why does Rossell claim that most bilingual education classes in the United States are really sheltered immersion classes?

3. What kind of classroom setting does the author believe is best suited to English language learners after one year in sheltered immersion programs?

During the last 25 years, U.S. public schools have developed six different instructional approaches to support students learning English as a second language:

- *Structured immersion*—or *sheltered English immersion*—provides instruction almost entirely in English, but in a self-contained classroom consisting only of English language learners (ELLs).

- *ESL pullout* programs supplement regular mainstream classroom instruction with instruction in a small-group setting outside the mainstream classroom aimed at developing English language skills.

- The *sink-or-swim* approach provides mainstream classroom instruction with no special help or scaffolding.

- *Transitional bilingual education* initially delivers instruction and develops students' literacy in the students' native language but puts a priority on developing students' English language skills.

- *Two-way bilingual education* (also known as *two-way immersion*) is designed to develop fluency in both the student's first language and a second language; teachers deliver instruction in both languages to classes consisting of both native English speakers and speakers of an-other language (most commonly Spanish).

- *Bilingual maintenance* programs generally consist of non-English speakers and, like two-way bilingual educa-tion programs, place equal emphasis on maintaining students' primary language and developing their En-glish proficiency.

Notice the order in which I have listed these programs. According to my own research and my reading of others' re-search, this list proceeds from the most effective to the least effective approaches in terms of helping students become pro-ficient at speaking, writing, and learning in English. This re-search indicates that in general, the most effective way for stu-dents to learn a second language and to learn subject matter in that second language is to learn *in* the second language—as in the first three programs—rather than learn in the students' native language, as in the last three programs. . . .

I am aware that this conclusion is highly controversial. In the past, bilingual education has enjoyed enormous support among many researchers and educators. But the apparently successful implementation of sheltered English immersion in California, Arizona, and Massachusetts may change the com-mon perception.

Teaching to the Needs of Immigrant Children

Despite the common belief in the effectiveness of bilingual education, my observations and my analyses of data from state department of education Web sites indicate that only a minority of immigrant children in the United States are en-rolled in bilingual programs in any form. In California, only about 29 percent of English language learners were enrolled in bilingual education in 1998, the year in which this approach was voted out as the default assignment for such students. Approximately 71 percent of California's English language learners participated in programs that used English as the dominant language of instruction—most of them in sink-or-swim or near-sink-or-swim situations. . . . Similarly, in Arizona in 2000 and in Massachusetts in 2002—the years in which these states mandated a switch to structured immersion—only 40 percent of English language learners at most were enrolled in bilingual education. . . .

Indeed, despite the lack of intellectual support for the sink-or-swim method, it seems to be the dominant approach to educating English language learners throughout the United States—perhaps because educators believe that the benefits of integration and language role modeling by fluent English speakers outweigh the disadvantages of students' initial non-comprehension of the curriculum, or perhaps because it is simply easier.

Another approach, sheltered English immersion (also called structured immersion), similarly predominates in more schools than one would assume from looking at statistical reports. A sheltered English immersion classroom differs from a mainstream, sink-or-swim classroom because the class is composed entirely of English language learners and is taught by a teacher trained in second-language acquisition techniques. The teacher conducts instruction almost exclusively in English, but at a pace students can keep up with.

Most Bilingual Classes Are Taught in English

Many programs throughout the United States identified as "bilingual education" can be more accurately described as sheltered English immersion because they are actually taught completely or almost completely in English. For example, during the two decades I have spent observing bilingual classrooms across the country, I have observed many Chinese "bilingual education" programs—but have never seen one taught in Chinese. Teachers in these classes believe that Chinese reading and writing skills are not transferable to English because the two written languages are so different. Teachers seldom even teach orally in Chinese because spoken Chinese encompasses many dialects, and it is rare that all students in a classroom speak the same one.

In fact, after observing numerous Russian, Vietnamese, Chinese, Khmer, Haitian, Cape Verdean, Spanish, Japanese, Hebrew, and Portuguese "bilingual education" classrooms and talking with their teachers, I have concluded that schools almost never offer bilingual education that fits the theoretical model, in which students learn to read and write initially as well as learn subject matter in their native language. The sole exception is in languages that use a Roman alphabet. If the primary language doesn't use the Roman alphabet, teachers perceive the transferability of reading skills as too small to justify the effort.

These practical reasons—ignored in the theoretical literature—account for the fact that in the United States, non-Spanish "bilingual education" programs are actually sheltered English immersion programs. This also means that statistics on bilingual education enrollment consistently overestimate the number of students who actually receive native language instruction.

Other Labels Applied

Sheltered English immersion also travels under other labels, such as *content ESL* [English as a second language] and, at the secondary level *sheltered subjects*. I once visited a school in New York City that, according to the board of education Web site, had a Bengali bilingual program. When I arrived at the classroom door, however, I found a sign that said *Content ESL*. In this classroom, Bengali speaking English language learners were taught by a teacher who was fluent in Bengali. Students who had little English fluency spent most of the day in this class learning English and learning subjects through English. The teacher taught no Bengali at all; he claimed that he did not even use it orally to clarify or explain. These students were actually in a sheltered English immersion class that tailored instruction to their needs.

At the secondary level, many students receive sheltered English immersion in the form of *sheltered subject* classes (such as sheltered algebra and sheltered U.S. history). Sheltered subject classes have been around for decades, but they often go unnoticed because the language of instruction is English and the curriculum is similar to that of a mainstream classroom. In a sheltered algebra class, for example, the teacher would teach algebra in English to a class composed solely of English language learners.

Although the literature specifies a number of ways in which sheltered English immersion classes differ from mainstream classes . . . I have observed many of these classrooms and have seen little difference between the two. Teachers in sheltered English immersion classes seem to speak no more slowly than those in mainstream classes do, and they do not use more visual props. The teachers tell me that the major difference is that they cover less material and use more repetition. Some of these sheltered classes are called "bilingual" if all the students have the same country of origin, but only Spanish speakers in secondary bilingual classes ever hear more than a minimal amount of their native language used in instruction.

Lessons from California

Although sheltered English immersion has been around for decades under various labels, it became the default assignment for English language learners by state mandate in California in 1998, in Arizona in 2000, and in Massachusetts in 2002. Research and observation in California yield some valuable insights about the ways in which teachers implement instruction for their English language learners and the relative effects of the bilingual education and sheltered immersion approaches. . . .

In response to the California law (Proposition 227), schools developed two structured immersion models that differ by the ethnic composition of the classrooms and by the amount of sheltering provided. Programs serving English language learners from a variety of linguistic backgrounds provide instruction and conversation in English only. Programs serving exclusively Spanish-speaking students, however, often use Spanish to explain or clarify concepts.

Because the school districts do not reliably distinguish between these different models, evaluating the academic impact of sheltered English immersion is difficult, if not impossible. We can, however, compare with some confidence the academic outcomes of keeping or dismantling transitional bilingual education because the California, Arizona, and Massachusetts laws all allow a school to offer bilingual education to students if the students' parents sign a waiver and if the school can justify using this approach on pedagogical or psychological grounds.

Bilingual Education Hampers Test Scores

Approximately 10 percent of English language learners in California are still enrolled in bilingual education. My analyses show . . . that after controlling for student and school characteristics, the average score increased by six points in reading and by three points in mathematics in schools that eliminated bilingual education. This is a .56 standard deviation gain in reading (a large effect) and a .21 standard deviation gain in math (a small effect). [V.] Bali (2001) found that taking Pasadena students out of bilingual education increased their reading scores by two points (.18 standard deviation) and their

An English Teacher's Endorsement

I've taught English in the South Bay [California] for several years. My most successful Hispanic students were those who had a good grounding in English from an early age. The earlier, the better. Their test scores proved the success of their learning English years before they reached high school. Their vocabulary was better, their written sentence structure was better and their comprehension of written materials was more quickly grasped.

Success ... can be summed up in two words: English immersion.

Robert Gillchrest,
"English Immersion for Spanish-Speakers,"
San Diego Union-Tribune, *October 19, 2008.*

math scores by one-half point (.03 standard deviation) compared with ELLs who had always been in English immersion classes.

Testing rates are another measure of the effectiveness of alternative programs because a lower testing rate means that the school considers more students unready to take the test. My research ... found that schools with more than 240 ELLs enrolled in bilingual education had lower testing rates in reading and math than did those with no ELLs enrolled in bilingual education, after controlling for student and school characteristics. Bali (2000) found that prior to 1998, the rate of testing for English language learners enrolled in bilingual education was 50 percent, compared with 89 percent for those enrolled in English language classrooms. Los Angeles Unified School District found that after five years of participating in the program, only 61 percent of ELLs enrolled in bilingual education were tested, compared with 97 percent of those in English language classrooms (1998).

The Move to the Mainstream Classroom

Unfortunately, there is no scientific research that directly compares the success rates of English language learners in a sheltered English immersion classroom with the success rates of ELLs in a mainstream classroom with ESL pullout. Nevertheless, I believed that at least for the first year, a sheltered classroom is a better environment for most English language learners than a mainstream classroom. My interviews in California indicated that teachers who formerly taught bilingual education but who now teach in sheltered English immersion programs believe the same.

After the first year, however, most English language learners are probably better off in mainstream classroom with some extra help. Most of them will know English well enough that a sheltered English immersion classroom would slow them down unnecessarily, particularly when new students without any English skills enter the class. The one-year time limit ("not normally intended to exceed one year") is part of the sheltered English immersion laws in California, Arizona, and Massachusetts and is a provision my fellow researcher and I recommended in our writing. . . .

Teacher Justification

My observations of almost 200 classrooms in California from spring 1999 through fall 2004 identified several themes that provide insight into the effectiveness of sheltered English immersion in the state.

Former Spanish bilingual education teachers were impressed by how quickly and eagerly their Spanish-speaking language learners in kindergarten and 1st grade learned to speak and read in English and how proud the students were of this accomplishment. The teachers were also surprised at how much they themselves liked teaching in sheltered English immersion classrooms, although they had never worked harder. . . .

When I asked the teachers in 2001 whether they would ever want to return to teaching in a bilingual education classroom, all of them said no. . . . Bilingual education was a good theory, they claimed, but in practice it had too many problems. They attributed these problems to a lack of materials, teachers, and support.

Interestingly, Chinese bilingual teachers saw Proposition 227 as a non-event. Because they had already been teaching in English, nothing had changed for them except that Proposition 227 justified their practices.

Besides moving most English language learners into sheltered immersion programs, Proposition 227 also changed the way Spanish bilingual education programs operated. The teachers with whom I spoke in the remaining Spanish bilingual education classes in spring 1999 said that they were using more English for instruction than they had in the past. They gave two reasons. First, the Proposition 227 vote expressed California's citizens' preference for a greater emphasis on English, and teachers believed that they should respond to the wishes of the people they served. Second, because the law greatly reduced the demand for bilingual classes, there was no guarantee in any specific school that a bilingual class could be assembled for the next grade in the following year. Accordingly, teachers felt the need to prepare their students for the possibility that they could soon be in an English language classroom. Thus, the task of comparing the effectiveness of bilingual education with that of sheltered immersion is further complicated by the fact that the former is less bilingual than it has been in the past.

English Instruction in Any Context Is Key

Despite the strong support for sheltered English immersion that now exists among educators, policymakers, and the public in California, only about half of all English language learners are actually enrolled in such programs. Most of the other half are in mainstream classrooms, and about 10 percent are still in bilingual education, albeit with more use of English than before.

My classroom observations in California indicate that most educators base decisions about how to teach not just on state mandates but also on their assessment of what their English language learners need, the numbers of English language learners in their classes, and their own philosophy. Most teachers with whom I have talked believe that teaching students in English is more important than ensuring that the students are in a sheltered environment (although the state law requires both).

In general, a mainstream classroom that provides extra help seems to be more practical for many schools, and any academic harm caused by such classrooms is apparently not significant enough to be noticeable to most educators or to offset the relative ease with which schools can form such classrooms. After all, most immigrant children in the United States and throughout the world are in mainstream classrooms, and most of them seem to swim, not sink.

"Native language and culture need to be respected in schools and used as the foundation for second language acquisition in order to ensure that [English language learners] receive a quality education."

English Immersion Education Is Flawed

Margaret Adams and Kellie M. Jones

In the following viewpoint, Margaret Adams and Kellie M. Jones argue that structured English immersion (SEI) programs are poorly executed in classrooms and are therefore a disservice to immigrant English language learners (ELLs). In the authors' opinion, SEI classes force ELLs to sink or swim with mainstream students, leaving many unable to comprehend basic curricula. Furthermore, Adams and Jones state that most mainstream teachers are not trained to treat the special linguistic needs of ELLs in their care. Without catering to the special learning needs of non-English-speaking students, SEI programs implemented in mainstream settings will likely fail students and communities, the authors assert. Margaret Adams is the former department

Margaret Adams and Kellie M. Jones, "Unmasking the Myths of Structured English Immersion: Why We Still Need Bilingual Educators, Native Language Instruction, and Incorporation of Home Culture," *Radical Teacher*, vol. 75, Spring 2006, pp. 16–21. Reproduced by permission.

head of the bilingual/ESL services at Brockton Primary Schools in Massachusetts. Kellie M. Jones is the current head of that department.

As you read, consider the following questions:

1. How was the SEI program originally designed to be implemented in Massachusetts schools, according to Adams and Jones?
2. As the authors report, what percent of Arizona ELLs were deemed proficient in English after only one year of SEI curriculum in 2003?
3. According to the authors, what has the loss of bilingual education teachers meant to school systems in SEI-mandated states?

Since November 2002, after a referendum vote referred to as Question 2 or "English for the Children," the education of English language learners (ELLs) in Massachusetts has been caught up in a chaotic whirlwind. Question 2, an initiative led by Californian businessman Ron Unz, mandated Structured English Immersion [SEI] as the only language program for ELLs, and the legislation included a provision for bringing suit against schools and districts willfully refusing to implement its provisions.

Born out of both ignorance and intent, the support that allowed for the passing of Question 2 paved the way for the rapid dismantling of bilingual programs. The referendum replaced the state law requiring Transitional Bilingual Education (TBE) in districts with 20 or more limited-English proficient students from the same language group. These programs have used native language materials and instruction to support content knowledge while developing students' English as a second language skills in both oral communication and literacy, and eventually transitioning them into all-English instruction.

It's interesting to note that the school systems' prompt response to the new legislation, in terms of program implementation, professional development, and the acquisition of new materials, in no way resembled the foot dragging and resistance that occurred when bilingual education (native language instruction) became the law in Massachusetts back in 1971.

English Immersion Supporters Misunderstand Language Acquisition

Structured English Immersion is vaguely defined as "nearly all classroom instruction is in English but with the curriculum and presentation designed for children who are learning the language" (Massachusetts Department of Education, 2003). It's thus not surprising that many misconceptions of what the law allows and does not allow have arisen and work against the best interests of ELLs. In the political rhetoric of having immigrant children learn English as quickly as possible, general principles of the developmental process of second language acquisition and valuing of diverse backgrounds have disappeared. Furthermore, we believe that one key factor contributing to the confusion is the reality that mainstream, English monolingual educators lack the necessary knowledge base for planning and implementing effective educational programming for ELLs.

As educators of ELLs and providers of professional development, we found ourselves in the dilemma of advocating for quality programming that meets the academic, social, and emotional needs of this population, while implementing a law and the SEI program model that are fundamentally flawed for their lack of understanding of complexities of language learning and the acculturation process of immigrant children. The purpose of this [viewpoint] is to discuss some of the dominant myths and misconceptions held by educators and their impact on linguistically diverse communities across the state as school districts struggle to implement this new law. Ultimately, our contention is that native language and culture need to be respected in schools and used as the foundation for second language acquisition in order to ensure that ELLs receive a quality education. However, putting much of the debate over bilingual education aside for the moment, let's simply look at what has been put into place and what is problematic about its implementation.

The Equivalent of "Sink or Swim" Submersion

The most common implementation of SEI has been to place students in mainstream classrooms where teachers do not modify their instruction to make it more comprehensible for ELLs. This type of instruction does not constitute Structured English Immersion. In fact, a mainstream classroom setting where the teacher instructs only in English without any special linguistic modifications constitutes what is known in the literature as "submersion" or "sink or swim." In this type of classroom, ELLs are left to their own devices to either quickly learn English and "swim" or fail to do so and thus "sink."

SEI is not intended to be the equivalent of submersion or "sink or swim." Even supporters of efforts to dismantle TBE envisioned SEI as being substantially different from mainstream classrooms. . . . The original conceptualization of SEI treated it as an instructional approach reserved for ELLs at an intermediate English language proficiency level with native language used to support students at early proficiency levels so that content knowledge would be more comprehensible. It is important to note that bilingual teachers in their capacity of native language and ESL instructors were effective users of sheltered English instruction prior to the passing of Question 2. In its ideal form, SEI refers to a thoughtfully designed language-sensitive instructional approach meant to assist ELLs in simultaneously acquiring English and grade-appropriate content area knowledge.

In the law, sheltered instruction is defined as classrooms where materials are in English and the curriculum is specifically design for ELLs (Massachusetts General Laws Chapter 71A). However, it is important to keep in mind that sheltered English instruction is an instructional methodology that simultaneously teaches English and content area knowledge and skills. In other words, SEI teachers develop their ELL students' English language abilities through linguistically modified instruction in the content areas such as math, science, and social studies. In SEI classrooms, teachers scaffold instruction using specific communication and text modification strategies to make English content comprehensible to ELL students with varying levels of English language proficiency.

Unrealistic Expectations

The reality is that ELLs require a well-developed English language development curriculum and program. To expect a mainstream math teacher to teach arithmetic while helping a newcomer conquer English, become literate, learn the material at hand, and prepare for a high-stakes test in order to advance and graduate is not realistic or fair to both teacher and ELL student.

Despite the original design of SEI, where ELLs are placed together, the common-sense belief that placing ELLs in classrooms with native English speakers will speed up the second language acquisition process continues to persist. In reality, when ELLs are placed in settings where teachers do not modify their instruction and practices, the results can be disastrous . . . as ELLs are prevented from meaningful access to instruction and curriculum because they cannot comprehend the teacher or instructional materials and demonstrate their content knowledge. ELLs submersed in mainstream classrooms are also unable to communicate effectively with native-English-speaking peers in the classroom. As a result, they are often relegated to an inferior status where they are placed in lower-level ability groups and taught through rote and discreet academic tasks that disregard the higher order thinking skills that native English speakers are taught. Clearly, a submersion "sink or swim" approach should not be the intent of the federal law or the ELL profession.

One Year Is Not Sufficient for English Proficiency

Despite the inappropriate wording of Question 2, stating that ELLs shall receive sheltered instruction for a temporary period "not normally intended to exceed one year", Title VI of the Federal Civil Rights Act does not permit time limitations placed on ELLs' English language acquisition (Massachusetts Department of Education, 2003). Title VI requires that ELLs be provided language support services until they are proficient enough in English to participate meaningfully in the district's mainstream education program. However, even those districts that service ELLs through appropriate SEI often violate the civil rights of ELLs by prematurely withdrawing needed language support and transitioning them into mainstream classrooms before they are sufficiently proficient in English.

Within the recent translation of SEI theory into practice, there is a pervasive myth that one year of English instruction via the content areas for all ELLs is sufficient. Perhaps the hidden (or not so hidden) ideology underlying this belief is another popular myth—prior immigrants had to do without and yet managed quickly and effortlessly to master English and academic success. In reality, in the 1900s, immigrants did not become proficient in English, nor did they have successful academic experiences in the United States, as evident in the large dropout rates during that time. . . . Historically, the successive generations were the ones who became proficient English speakers.

Despite the potential effectiveness of SEI and its numerous implementations, it has failed to live up to English-only proponents' false claim that ELLs can reach full English language proficiency in one year's time. In fact, the magical accelerated language teaching attributes associated with SEI by its proponents are unsupported by statewide English proficiency test results for the 2004–2005 school year. The test results showed that after one year of SEI instruction, the majority of ELL students still remained at a beginning English proficiency level (Massachusetts Department of Education, 2005a). Similarly, the state standards-based assessment in English language arts and mathematics—the Massachusetts Comprehensive Assessment System (MCAS)—showed that over the past four years there has been little improvement in the scores of ELLs. For example, one third of fourth grade ELLs failed the MCAS and one half fell into the "needs improvement" level (Massachusetts Department of Education, 2005b).

The touted "one-year SEI miracle" has also failed to materialize in California and Arizona where similar English-only mandates have been passed. In California, where SEI has been in effect since 1998, the reclassification of English language proficiency and academic performance of ELLs has remained relatively unchanged. . . . The same scenario is evident in Arizona, where in 2003, only 11% of ELLs were deemed proficient in English after one year of SEI. . . . One might argue that English proficiency for ELLs will take even longer than under more effective bilingual programs that utilize students' native language to support their English development; so why implement it at the expense of nurturing the development of bilingual and biliterate children?

Losing Valuable Resources

The provisions of Question 2 undervalue the powerful role of a teacher who shares a common language and culture with an ELL. Since the law mandated that academic instruction be overwhelmingly in English, many districts felt that TBE teachers were no longer needed. As a consequence, most bilingual

An Impression of Success

Even if we were to focus only on academic achievement ... properly funded, accountable bilingual education is the educational choice. Research consistently shows that, yes, children can learn "survival English" in one to three years. So children can give the impression in immersion programs of success—early on. But when the content comes into play, those children far underperform because they don't comprehend the academic language necessary to compete.

Jo Beth Jimerson,
"Bilingual Education a Better Choice Than Immersion,"
My SA Opinion, February 11, 2008. www.mysanantonio.com.

teachers were either reassigned or laid off as districts saw an opportunity to reconcile shrinking school budgets and/or get rid of teachers perceived as unnecessary and incapable of teaching in structured English classrooms. One argument that has been made is that the abolition of bilingual education and the dismissal of bilingual teachers effectively eliminated numerous minority power holders in school districts. The end result is that fewer minority educators hold positions of authority within districts across the state. Those who remained were placed in SEI classrooms and little effort has been made to capitalize on these teachers' expertise and strengths especially in the development of new SEI programs.

With the elimination of previously well-prepared bilingual teachers, schools now have no additional resources to facilitate the needed communication with newly arrived students and their families. The powerful role played by the TBE teacher in facilitating the families' acculturation to the American educational system and supporting newcomers through the initial stages of cultural shock has been lost. Currently, teachers across the state scream for aid in communicating with non-English speaking families since the teachers are monolinguals and cannot speak a language other than English. Many parents consequently shy away from coming to school events and parent-teacher conferences even though they are invited. In California, English monolingual teachers of ELLs report the need to communicate and connect with families and students as one of their major concerns. . . .

Despite the perception that Question 2 completely outlawed native language use, the law actually permits that native languages may be used for clarification purposes allowing for "minimal amount of the child's native language when necessary" (Massachusetts General Laws Chapter 71 A). But who is going to do this clarifying in the native language when bilingual teachers are no longer available? . . .

Minimal Teacher Training for New SEI Teachers

Currently, the majority of ELLs in Massachusetts are now in mainstream classrooms and, as a result, all teachers have become responsible for the academic and linguistic achievement of ELLs. With the increased need to prepare English monolingual teachers, districts have responded by increasing minimal teacher training and inservice efforts. The belief is that with a little bit of training, teachers can effectively meet the needs of ELLs.

In the past, bilingual education and ESL licensure required a master's degree from programs that provided graduate students with training and expertise on topics such as linguistics, sociolinguistics, methodologies, first and second language acquisition theories, culturally relevant teaching, and use of culturally and linguistically appropriate assessments. Ironically, it is precisely at this moment in time when ELLs are being placed in classrooms with monolingual teachers lacking knowledge needed for working effectively with ELLs that the Massachusetts Department of Education has elected to reduce the teacher training knowledge base to four categories and approximately 75 hours of training. Instead of graduate-level courses on language acquisition and culture competence, the Massachusetts Department of Education now only requires 10 hours of preparation. In addition, only 20–25 hours is required for the teaching of reading and writing to ELLs (Massachusetts Department of Education, 2004b). A similar scenario is occurring in Arizona through the creation of an "SEI endorsement" that requires only 60 hours of training beyond the original teacher certification. . . .

Even with some professional development, mainstream teachers still feel ill prepared to meet the needs of ELLs in their classrooms. Once teachers understand the complexities of second language learning and are introduced to the distinctions between social language and academic language, they realize the limitations of their knowledge base. . . .

In addition, all the research indicates that in order for teachers to effectively incorporate new practices into their teaching, sustained professional development is needed. One-step training without follow-up constitutes the least effective form of professional development. Ongoing training accompanied by coaching and modeling opportunities constitutes a much more effective model. . . .

ELLs Are Not a Priority

The promised silver-lining of Question 2—that all teachers would be appropriately prepared to effectively teach ELLs, and that linguistic-minority children would be positioned to succeed—has not been delivered. Instead, what seems to be occurring is the further deterioration of ELL education, all in the name of "English for the children." It's awful to think and yet necessary to contemplate the possibility that this was the goal in the first place—that Unz never intended his initiatives to work in the best interest of linguistic-minority children or their families. While we may never know the answer to this question, regardless, current efforts to water down the preparation of SEI teachers, to perpetuate the common myths/misconceptions about language acquisition and teaching, and the absolute misuse of SEI all point to the sad reality that the education of linguistic-minority students under current mandates is simply not a priority. If anything, the priority seems to be focused on accommodating English monolingual teachers who happen to work with ELL students. Every effort is being made for English monolingual teachers to teach as usual and have ELLs accommodate their teachers' lack of training and English monolingualism and not the other way around. This situation would be found to be absurd and intolerable if the students were considered to be high status students. But since they are not, it is perfectly acceptable to miseducate them both linguistically and academically.

Periodical Bibliography

The following articles have been selected to supplement the diverse views presented in this chapter.

Susan Black	"Easing ESL Students into Learning English Well," *Education Digest*, September 2005.
District Administration	"Speakers Against Learners," January 2008.
Kendra Hamilton	"Bilingual or Immersion?" *Diverse: Issues in Higher Education*, April 20, 2006.
Sarah Karlin	"The Invisible Class," *American School Board Journal*, November 2007.
K.C. McAlpin	"McCain Should Pledge to Make English Official Language," *Human Events*, July 14, 2008.
Zach Miners	"English Language Learners," *District Administration*, August 2008.
Jo Anna Patton	"You're Not Bilingual, So What?" *Library Media Connection*, April/May 2008.
Pilar Pinedo	"The Best of Both Worlds," *NEA Today*, May 2007.
Leticia Salais	"Saying 'Adiós' to Spanglish," *Newsweek*, December 17, 2007.
Mary Ann Zehr	"NAEP Scores in States That Cut Bilingual Ed. Fuel Concern on ELLs," *Education Week*, May 14, 2008.

OPPOSING
VIEWPOINTS®
SERIES

CHAPTER 3

How Should the United States Deter Illegal Immigration?

Chapter Preface

In April 2005, Chris Simcox, an Arizonan, and Jim Gilchrest of California launched the Minuteman Project by calling upon volunteers to show their commitment to stemming the tide of illegal immigrants crossing the porous and poorly monitored Arizona-Mexico border. Simcox and Gilchrest succeeded in drawing over 900 senior citizens, retired police officers and firefighters, military veterans, and other concerned citizens to the cause. They were stationed every half-mile along the border region where illegals were known to cross. The volunteers were not armed and were given instructions not to confront immigrants but only report on their whereabouts so that authorities could take appropriate action.

According to Minuteman spokespersons, the month-long monitoring efforts led to the apprehension of 330 border crossers. It was a victory that the group touted in the media— and one that jump-started other Minuteman initiatives in other states and led to political rallies bringing attention to the problem of illegal immigration. "It has moved into politics on the local, state and federal level, what we hope is in every district in this country," Simcox said. "We mean business." In 2006, the group organized a political caravan to Washington D.C. to bring pressure on President George W. Bush to take action on the issue. Bush had already consented to add more border patrol agents to the region, but he remained adamantly against citizens taking monitoring responsibilities into their own hands. "I am against vigilantes in the United States of America. . . . I am for enforcing the law in a rational way," Bush stated.

Over time, the Minutemen organization splintered and suffered both infighting and accusations of financial mismanagement. Opponents of the movement paint the Minutemen as extremists. State Senator Juan Hinojosa of Texas told reporters, "I don't think that there's any doubt that there's a tinge of racism beneath the surface in their attempt to try to stop immigrants from Mexico." Even the U.S. border agents have referred to the civilian volunteers as a nuisance to their patrolling efforts. Supporters of the Minuteman movement see it as a form of patriotism. They contend the border duty is necessary given that, in their opinion, the government is not assuming its responsibilities. The Campo, California, branch of the organization, for example, bears the motto "Doing for our country what our government won't."

Whether popular or not, the Minuteman movement illustrates one way in which Americans are responding to the issue of illegal immigration. The viewpoints in this chapter explore other controversial plans and programs the United States is using to control borders and deter illegal immigrants.

"Border fencing has proven to be an effective enforcement tool with verifiable results."

A Border Fence Will Deter Illegal Immigration

Duncan Hunter

In the following viewpoint, Duncan Hunter, a California Representative to the U.S. Congress, advocates the completion of a border fence along the U.S.-Mexico border. Hunter explains that the stretch of fencing on the border near San Diego is already reducing the flow of illegal aliens and the narcotics trade in the area. He expects that extending the fence across 854 miles of borderlands will yield similar results and help secure the homeland from intrusion by terrorists who are well aware of the weaknesses of the southern border.

As you read, consider the following questions:

1. How much of the 854 miles of fencing did the Department of Homeland Security (DHS) concede to build, according to Hunter?

2. As Hunter claims, how many non-Mexican nationals were apprehended crossing the U.S.-Mexico border in 2005?

Duncan Hunter, "If We Build It They Won't Come," *Human Events*, vol. 63, May 22, 2007. Copyright © 2007 Human Events Inc. Reproduced by permission.

3. How much money did the DHS have on hand to commit to the border fence project in 2007, as Hunter states?

It's much tougher than it should be to secure America's borders. While the technology and manpower are all within reach, what seems beyond our grasp is the ability to act. Take [the 2006] legislation calling for construction of 854 miles of fence on our Southern border.

It's all too obvious that America is under threat because its land borders are largely porous and unprotected. In response [in 2006] Congress passed, and the President [George W. Bush] signed into law, legislation calling for the construction of those 854 miles of border fencing along the U.S.-Mexico border. Despite this legislative mandate by the U.S. Congress, the Department of Homeland Security [DHS] [in 2007] announced its intention to build only 370 miles of fencing along the border, not the 854 miles required by the legislation.

This directive, despite its clarity, appears to have been interpreted as a suggestion. It is not: it's the law—and the border fence must be built.

Fencing Is an Effective Deterrent

The Secure Fence Act requires that reinforced fencing and related infrastructure be installed along the most dangerous and problematic smuggling corridors along our Southern land border, which continue providing illegal immigrants, drug smugglers and potential terrorist access into the United States. As the original author of the measure's fencing provision, I expected there to be some opposition to implementing strategic fencing along our land border with Mexico. I did not, however, expect one of the biggest obstacles to be the federal agency primarily responsible for protecting the American homeland, especially when border fencing has proven to be an effective enforcement tool with verifiable results.

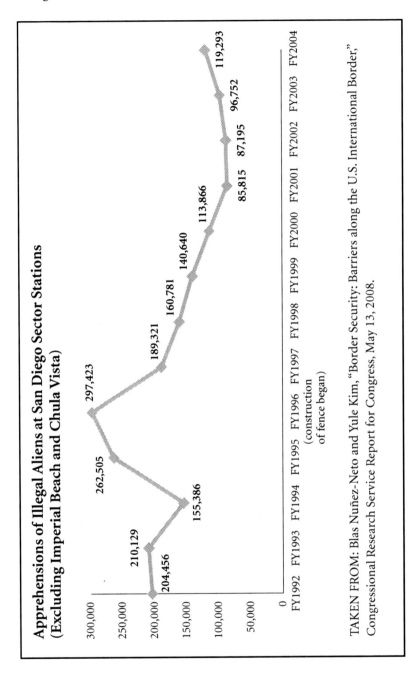

Apprehensions of Illegal Aliens at San Diego Sector Stations (Excluding Imperial Beach and Chula Vista)

- FY1992: 204,456
- FY1993: 210,129
- FY1994: 262,505
- FY1995: 297,423
- FY1996: 189,321
- FY1997: 160,781
- FY1998: 140,640
- FY1999: 113,866
- FY2000: 155,386 (construction of fence began)
- FY2001: 85,815
- FY2002: 87,195
- FY2003: 96,752
- FY2004: 119,293

TAKEN FROM: Blas Nuñez-Neto and Yule Kim, "Border Security: Barriers along the U.S. International Border," Congressional Research Service Report for Congress, May 13, 2008.

In San Diego County, for example, border fencing remains a critical part of our continuing effort to address the problems commonly associated with illegal immigration. Since construction of the San Diego Border Fence began in 1996, the smuggling of people and narcotics has dropped drastically, crime rates have been reduced by half according to FBI statistics, vehicle drug drive-throughs have been eliminated and apprehensions have decreased as the result of fewer crossing attempts.

The [Bill] Clinton Administration opposed the construction of the San Diego Border Fence as a method of closing the prolific smuggling corridor that once existed between San Diego and Tijuana, Mexico. The Clinton Administration, however, also recognized its responsibility under the law. Construction of the San Diego Border Fence began and conditions on both sides of the border immediately improved.

The Bush Administration says it remains committed to securing the border. I intend to hold them to their word. Just as I did with the Clinton Administration, I will continue reminding the Bush Administration of their obligation under the law to build the border fence. I believe they can, and will, do better.

A Homeland Security and Immigration Concern

Bureaucracy is rarely ever capable of producing immediate results. But when it threatens the safety and security of our communities, it becomes intolerable. The decision not to build fencing as dictated by law can only serve to demonstrate that we are not serious about securing our borders and enforcing our nation's immigration laws.

Why is reinforced border infrastructure necessary? In 2005, 155,000 foreign nationals from countries other than Mexico were apprehended attempting to cross our land border with Mexico. Alarmingly, many of these individuals originated from countries of national security concern, including Syria, Iran, Lebanon and Yemen, and likely represent only a fraction of those who successfully entered our country without the knowledge of border security officials or the consent of our government.

It has also been reported that several of the individuals who were discovered to be plotting the next major terrorist attack against the United States, targeting soldiers at Fort Dix, crossed the U.S.-Mexico border through Brownsville, Texas. Whether they entered as children or adults, the fact that they originated from countries far from our shores demonstrates that across the world, it is understood that the best way to illegally enter the United States is through our land border with Mexico.

Time to Get Serious

[As of May 2007], only 12 miles of the 854 miles of border fencing called for in the Secure Fence Act have been constructed. While it's a start, the 370 miles of fencing promised by DHS represents a significant departure from what's required by federal law. Let's be perfectly clear: it's not enough. Even the 854 miles of fence legislated last year is only a beginning. Legislation . . . under consideration [in 2007] by the U.S. Senate to reform our immigration system also reaffirms DHS's decision to only build 370 miles of fencing. This legislation is weak on enforcement, comprehensively fails to make border security a priority and wrongly retreats from the mandates of the Secure Fence Act.

We know from our experiences in San Diego that border fencing works and when extended across Arizona, New Mexico and Texas, it will have the same salutary effect. DHS has more than $1 billion cash on hand for border fence construction and more will surely be delivered. It's time we get serious about border control, do what's right, and build the border fence. Secure borders make America safer. What's so hard to understand about that?

"Migrants intent on crossing the border will repeatedly try to do so—often successfully—no matter the obstacles in their way."

A Border Fence Will Not Deter Illegal Immigration

Melanie Mason

Melanie Mason is a journalist who has written for The New Republic. *In the following viewpoint from that news source, Mason argues that a border fence along the U.S.-Mexico border will not stop illegal aliens because most immigrants use legal ports to enter America. She states that the proposed fencing project is extremely expensive, can be damaging to the environment, and will fail to deter those immigrants who are intent on entering the country.*

As you read, consider the following questions:

1. As Mason states, what percent of immigrants who were apprehended on their most recent attempt to cross the border eventually succeeded in entering on later attempts?

2. How will a border fence likely worsen the problem it was meant to solve, in Mason's view?

3. As the author explains, what did the Congressional Research Service estimate the total cost of the proposed border fence would be over its 25-year life span?

In this political season [i.e., the presidential race in 2008], immigration is the issue that everyone's taking pains *not* to discuss. The presidential candidates are merely paying the same lip service to border security. Congress has all but abandoned comprehensive immigration reform, and the [George W.] Bush administration continues to pile all their immigration-policy eggs in the border-security basket. But that doesn't mean nothing is happening. Homeland Security [DHS] head Michael Chertoff, in an April [2008] trip to the U.S.-Mexico border, made clear his determination that 670 miles of border fence, already under construction in Arizona and California, be completed by the end of the year. The border fence project has faced embarrassments—illegal immigrants employed to build the wall, a "Virtual Fence" project that cannot distinguish humans and vehicles from livestock and bushes—but those setbacks pale in comparison to its fundamental flaws. Below [are] six simple reasons a fence spanning the U.S.-Mexico border is bad policy.

It Does Not Work

Most experts say that physical fencing would not drastically decrease the number of illegal immigrants entering the country. The Pew Hispanic Center estimates that as much as 40–50 percent of the U.S.'s unauthorized migrant population entered the country through legal ports of entry, either with nonimmigrant visas that subsequently expired (known as "overstayers") or by using a Border Crossing Card that allows for short visits to the border region. A fence spanning the border would not prevent their entry to the country. And there is little evidence that a fence would be a successful deterrent to other would-be border crossers. In a survey done by Wayne Cornelius, director of the Center for Comparative Immigration Studies at UC San Diego, 90 percent of respondents who intended to migrate to the United States were aware that border crossing was "very dangerous," but this failed to discourage them from their plans. Apprehensions by the border patrol do little to dissuade repeat border-crossing attempts. In Cornelius' survey of migrants from the Mexican state of Oaxaca, 48 percent were apprehended on their most recent trip to the border. 96 percent of those migrants were able to enter eventually. Migrants intent on crossing the border will repeatedly try to do so—often successfully—no matter the obstacles in their way.

It Exacerbates the Problem

Prior to the increase in border enforcement, many unauthorized migrants from Mexico followed a circulatory migration pattern, where mostly male migrants would spend part of the year in the United States, performing seasonal jobs or short-term work. They would often return for holidays, and their families tended to remain in Mexico. As border crossings have become more difficult, the rate of return among unauthorized migrants has decreased. Audrey Singer, an immigration expert with the Brookings Institution, explains that "more men are staying, women are coming and families are consolidating on this side of the border." Also compounding this consolidation within the U.S. is the increased use of smugglers to facilitate border crossings. From 2005–2007, 80 percent of undocumented migrants used smugglers, known as "coyotes," to help them across the border, according to Cornelius. With coyotes' fees at several thousand dollars and growing, migrants are unlikely to make circular trips across the border using coyotes and are therefore more inclined to stay in the U.S. permanently. Douglas Massey, professor of sociology at Princeton University, sums it up: "The ultimate effect of the border fence policy is to increase the size [of the undocumented population] and to make it more permanent."

Explaining the Slowdown in Illegal Immigration

The fence is undoubtedly changing patterns of illegal immigration. But is it staunching the flow? The Border Patrol points to the fact that they are catching fewer people. Yet this is a very imperfect measure, rather like estimating the number of fish in the sea from those hauled up in fishermen's nets. The figures do not count those who make it, and they double-count people who keep trying. Remittances to Mexico provide a better picture. These were rising until recently, largely because immigrants began to send more money through formal channels. Now they are falling, but not by much. . . .

There is a more obvious reason for the recent slowdown in illegal immigration. Construction and landscaping jobs, a common source of employment for Latino immigrants both legal and illegal, have disappeared as the housing market has collapsed. In the past year [2008] the Hispanic unemployment rate has risen from 5.4% to 8.0%. Among Hispanics aged 16 to 19 the rate is 22.8%. This deters would-be workers from crossing the border and curtails the ability of people already in America to pay for their relatives to make the trip.

Economist,
"Good Neighbors Make Fences," October 2, 2008.

It Is Inhumane

Major border enforcement operations have focused on urban areas, where border crossers have only a short distance to traverse. With increased enforcement, people have, according to Singer, abandoned these "institutionalized crossing patterns" and moved to places with "harsher climate, harsher terrain, and a greater likelihood of injury and death." Deaths along the border have increased substantially since the mid-1990s—500 fatalities in 2007 alone. According to Cornelius, "women and children are overrepresented in fatalities, in proportion to their numbers among clandestine entrants. In several recent years, about 18 percent of the fatalities have been women and minors under 18."

It Is Enormously Costly

Though the exact figure is a matter of some dispute, there's no disagreement that a fence would be a tremendous expense. The Congressional Budget Office predicts $3 million per mile in construction cost. The Department of Homeland Security estimates that the San Diego portion of the fence alone would cost $127 million for a length of 14 miles, roughly $9 million per mile. Factoring in repairs and maintenance, the Congressional Research Service estimates that a 25-year life span of a 700-mile fence (far short of the entire 1,952-mile border) would cost up to $49 billion.

It Is Environmentally Damaging

The border region is an environmentally sensitive area, providing for numerous imperiled species. The fence proposed by the Secure Fence Act of 2006 would cross multiple protected federal lands. Biologists worry that jaguars, extremely rare in the United States, would see their cross-border migration patterns disrupted, threatening their survival. To see how a fence may negatively affect environmentally valuable land, one needs only look to the state of limbo facing the Sabal Palm Audubon Center in Brownsville, Texas. If DHS has its way, a border fence constructed to the north of this bird sanctuary would essentially cede the land to Mexico, upsetting conservationists and ecotourism promoters alike. Michael Chertoff's recent waiver of more than 30 environmental and land-management laws means that DHS will not have to examine in detail the fence's effects on wildlife, water quality, and vegetation prior to construction.

It Is Legally Dubious

Chertoff's ability to waive those laws is derived from a 2005 law passed by Congress that allowed the Secretary of Homeland Security to waive "all legal requirements" in order to speed up the construction [of] the fence. The bill sharply limits judicial review to a single District judge; any appeal from that ruling can only go to the Supreme Court at the Court's discretion. The Supreme Court recently declined to hear a challenge from the Sierra Club and Defenders of Wildlife. Both organizations, along with *New York Times* columnist Adam Liptak, argue that Congress's voluntary delegation powers to the executive branch threatens the basic Constitutional principle of separation of powers. Oliver Bernstein, a spokesman for Sierra Club, told the *Los Angeles Times* that the Supreme Court's hands-off approach "leaves one man—the secretary of the Homeland Security—with the extraordinary power to ignore any and all of the laws designed to protect the American people, our lands and our natural resources."

So, if not a fence, then what? Most experts on all sides of the immigration debate agree that the border fence is a political band-aid for a larger policy problem. Mark Krikorian of the restrictionist Center for Immigration Studies believes that "politicians tend to over-emphasize the importance of fencing." Cecilia Muñoz, of the Hispanic advocacy group National Council of La Raza calls the fence a "monument to Congress's efforts to look like they're doing something." The enforcement-first approach of the Bush administration does nothing to deal with the 12 million undocumented immigrants already in this country, or American employers' demand for cheap immigrant labor, or the lack of a legal path for entry for future immigrants. Ways of dealing with this demand can—and should—be debated, but let's cease to delude ourselves that this fence offers the answer.

> *"It is possible that an eventual manda-tory use of E-Verify by all businesses could eliminate nearly all of the 'on-the-books' employment of illegal immi-grants in the U.S."*

Employment Verification Will Deter Illegal Immigration

Robert E. Rector

Welfare expert Robert Rector contends in the following viewpoint that checking the eligibility of employees through electronic veri-fication will help reduce the amount of illegal immigration in the United States. According to Rector, the E-Verify process will provide law-abiding employers with a tool to keep undocu-mented workers off their payrolls, and in turn, by denying em-ployment, the system will deter illegal immigrants from seeking jobs in America. In Rector's view, electronic verification is a valuable asset to immigration control because it is remarkably accurate, and it is relatively inexpensive for the government to operate. Robert Rector is a senior research fellow at The Heritage Foundation, a conservative public policy think tank.

Robert Rector, "Reducing Illegal Immigration Through Employment Verification, En-forcement, and Protection," *Heritage Foundation Backgrounder*, vol. 2192, October 7, 2008, pp. 1–6, 10–12. Copyright © 2008 The Heritage Foundation. Reproduced by per-mission.

As you read, consider the following questions:

1. What government departments run the E Verify system, as Rector reports?

2. As Rector writes, what percent of illegal employment takes place "on the books" and thus can be reduced by electronic verification?

3. How much money per year will the E-Verify system cost each American household in its initial four-year start-up phase, according to Rector?

Immigration reform has many facets: It must protect national security, uphold the rule of law, strengthen citizenship, and benefit the American economy. The overall effect must be to reduce illegal immigration into the United States. Although border security generally receives more attention, serious enforcement of current laws prohibiting the employment of illegals is also an important tool in an overall strategy to reduce illegal immigration.

The majority of persons who enter the U.S. illegally or unlawfully overstay temporary visas do so for purposes of employment. Employment of such individuals has been illegal since 1986, although that law has never been seriously enforced. If access to employment were curtailed in accord with that law, many (probably even a large majority) of current illegal immigrants would leave the country voluntarily, and the number of future illegal entrants would be greatly reduced.

Since employment is the magnet that draws illegal immigrants into the U.S., it follows that the best way to reduce illegal immigration is to shrink the employment magnet. To accomplish this without resorting to the method of routinely rounding up and deporting thousands of illegal workers only to have them return and obtain another readily available job, policy should focus on the businesses that hire illegal immigrants and let general employment rules rather than individual arrests drive the reduction in illegal immigration.

The policy should be based on the principles of *empowerment, deterrence,* and *information.* It should empower honest employers by giving them the tools to determine quickly and accurately whether a new hire is an authorized worker. It should hold employers free from penalty if they inadvertently hire an illegal worker after following the prescribed procedures.

Further, the policy should empower honest employers by freeing them from the burden of competing with dishonest businesses that deliberately hire illegal workers. This means that it must deter dishonest employers who willfully employ unverified and unlawful workers by imposing substantial penalties on the employers when such hiring occurs. For deterrence to work, however, both the government and employers must have timely and accurate information regarding new hires.

The most promising solution to this problem is a tool called E-Verify. A real-time, Web-based verification system run by the Department of Homeland Security (DHS) and the Social Security Administration (SSA), E-Verify can determine with great accuracy the authenticity of the personal information and credentials offered by new hires. In most cases, verification occurs almost instantly.

With the improvements suggested in this [viewpoint] and those ongoing refinements to the existing program, E-Verify can be highly effective in reducing the employment of illegal immigrants. It is possible that an eventual mandatory use of E-Verify by all businesses could eliminate nearly all of the "on-the-books" employment of illegal immigrants in the U.S.—an estimated 4 million illegal workers.

Congress should reauthorize E-Verify as it currently exists and work to expand its reach and efficacy significantly in recognition of the fact that the law prohibits employers from hiring illegal immigrants and that the objective of E-Verify is to enforce that law.

This approach, combined with targeted enforcement and stiff penalties for those who do not comply with verification requirements, will significantly deter unlawful employment and thereby reduce the demand for illegal workers. That will, in turn, reduce the chief incentive of those seeking to enter the United States illegally.

Understanding the Employment of Illegal Immigrants

By most estimates, around 8 million illegal immigrants work in the U.S. There are generally three means by which illegal aliens obtain employment.

1. Working "on the books" with a fictitious Social Security number. In this situation, the illegal alien is employed formally by a business, just as any other employee is. The employer withholds Social Security (FICA) taxes and files a W-2 tax form for the employee. The illegal employee presents identity documents to the employer showing that he is either a U.S. citizen or lawful immigrant entitled to work.

   These documents will contain a name, date of birth, Social Security number, and possibly a green card number, which are either partially or completely fictitious. The employer dutifully records this fictitious information on an official form called an I-9 and stores the form in a file cabinet. If the information on the I-9 were checked, it would immediately be found to be fraudulent; at present, however, there is no practical means for the government to corroborate the information on the I-9.

2. Working "on the books" through identity fraud. In this situation, the illegal alien is also employed by a business just like any other employee. The employer withholds

Social Security (FICA) taxes and files a W-2 tax form for the employee. The illegal employee presents identity documents to the employer showing that he is either a U.S. citizen or lawful immigrant entitled to work.

However, in this case, the name, date of birth, Social Security number and (in some cases) green card number on the documents correspond to the identity of a real U.S. citizen or lawful immigrant. To obtain employment, the illegal fraudulently assumes the identity of another real person. The employer records the fraudulent information on the I-9 and keeps the I-9 on file, but neither the employer nor the government checks to determine whether the employee is the person he purports to be.

3. Working "off the books." In this situation, the employer deliberately conceals the employment of the illegal alien from the government. There is no public record of the employee, no W-4 withholding form is filed, FICA taxes are not paid, and no W-2 statement is sent to the government. It is very unlikely that an I-9 form is completed or kept.

Of the millions of illegal immigrants in this country, the best evidence suggests that some 50 percent to 60 percent of this employment occurs "on the books." It is unclear how much "on-the-books" employment of illegal aliens is done with fictitious information and how much is done by identity fraud.

To reduce illegal immigration, all three means of illegal employment must be addressed, but this need for a broad approach should not be used as an excuse to do nothing. Although it is true that reducing "off-the-books" employment will be the most difficult task, that does not mean that the government should do little or nothing about the high levels of "on-the-books" illegal employment until it has devised a

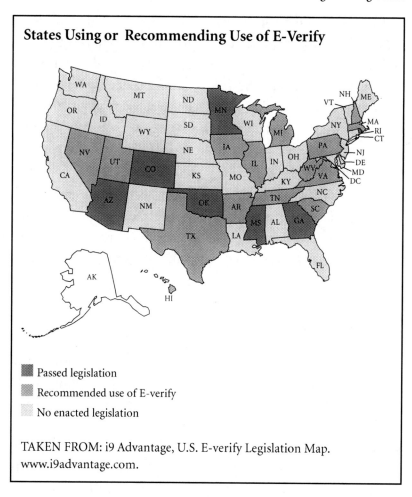

States Using or Recommending Use of E-Verify

■ Passed legislation

▨ Recommended use of E-verify

░ No enacted legislation

TAKEN FROM: i9 Advantage, U.S. E-verify Legislation Map.
www.i9advantage.com.

foolproof means of stopping underground employment as
well. Proper policy should take the critical first step of controlling "on-the-books" employment of illegal aliens. . . .

How E-Verify Works

E-Verify is a Web-based electronic verification system operated
by the Department of Homeland Security and the Social Security Administration that allows employers to check instantly
the authenticity of identity information provided by new employees. In general, the employer will use a personal computer

117

to submit certain basic information concerning the employee (name, date of birth, Social Security number, etc.) to the government. The information is securely transmitted to DHS and SSA, and DHS checks the information to determine whether it corresponds to a U.S. citizen or to a work-eligible immigrant. In most cases, DHS can check and confirm the employee information and transmit a definitive reply to the employer within seconds.

The E-Verify system thus provides a very quick and largely accurate check of the authenticity of information presented by newly hired employees. The system also provides a simple and rapid mechanism to correct initial erroneous determinations. . . .

Remarkable Accuracy of the System

In 2007, Westat, an influential private research firm located in Rockville, Maryland, conducted a formal evaluation of E-Verify and its predecessor, Basic Pilot, for the DHS. As part of this evaluation, Westat reviewed all 2.7 million employee submissions to Basic Pilot/E-Verify between October 2005 and March 2007. The Westat evaluation provides the most thorough information currently available on the operation of E-Verify.

- During that period, 92 percent of submissions received an initial positive confirmation; around 1 percent of submissions received an initial tentative non-confirmation that was contested and converted into a final positive confirmation once information discrepancies were corrected; and around 7 percent of submissions resulted in final non-confirmations, nearly all resulting from initial tentative non-confirmations that were never contested.

- Among all employees who were eventually found to be work-authorized, 99.4 percent received an initial positive confirmation, and 0.6 percent received an initial tentative non-confirmation that was corrected by a brief visit to an SSA or USCIS [United States Citizen and Immigration Service] office.

- Among individuals found to be native-born citizens, 99.9 percent received an initial positive confirmation, and 0.1 percent received an initial tentative non-confirmation that was quickly corrected.

- Among work-authorized, foreign-born individuals, 97 percent received an initial positive confirmation, and 3 percent received an initial tentative non-confirmation that was quickly corrected.

Overall, the evaluation showed that E-Verify was very successful in distinguishing between authorized and unauthorized workers. As noted, 7 percent of submissions to E-Verify resulted in final non-confirmations; the Westat evaluation estimated that 95 percent of these final non-confirmations were, in fact, unauthorized workers seeking employment. If used widely, the system has the potential to block nearly all employment based on fictitious identities.

On the other hand, the Westat report estimated that 5 percent of final non-confirmations under the system may have been authorized workers. These misidentified workers represented about one of every 300 persons reviewed by E-Verify. The Westat evaluation reported no instances in which authorized workers who received a tentative non-confirmation were unable to contest the ruling successfully and establish proper work authorization. Instead, the misidentified workers were individuals who received an erroneous initial tentative non-confirmation but failed, for a variety of reasons, to contest that ruling. . . .

Costs to Government of Expanding E-Verify

Currently, E-Verify is used to check less than one-tenth of total new hires in the U.S. If it were used for all new hires each year, the cost to government to operate the system would rise, with most of the added costs occurring in USCIS. This agency has estimated that a phased four-year expansion of E-Verify resulting in the ongoing coverage of all new hires in the fourth year would cost $765 million over the four-year period. Coverage of all new hires and current employees in four years would cost $838 million, or an average of $210 million per year.

Expansion of E-Verify use would also result in added costs to SSA because extra staff would be needed to process the increase in contested "tentative non-confirmations." SSA has estimated that a phased expansion to cover all current employees and all new hires annually would cost it $281 million over five years, or $55 million per year.

In total, then, the cost to government of implementing universal E-Verify coverage would be around $1 billion over four years. This amounts to about $2.50 per U.S. household per year.

Additional government expenditures might be required to meet the costs of prosecuting employers who willfully disregarded the E-Verify system by employing workers found to be unauthorized; however, fines on such employers could offset some or all of this enforcement cost. . . .

Broad-Based Verification Is Needed

Some suggest that employment of illegal immigrants is focused in a few industries and that it is therefore unnecessary to establish employment verification across the entire economy. Instead, a policy of targeted verification and enforcement in those particular industries will suffice to effect significant reductions in illegal immigration. This argument falls apart when one examines the facts.

Though illegal immigrants are disproportionately low-skilled, they are spread widely through the economy. Illegal immigrants appear to work most commonly in six industries (in order of descending scale): construction, restaurants, land-scaping, janitorial services, food processing, and hotels. In fact, only around half of illegals work in these industries. Some 45 percent may be visa overstayers rather than unlawful border crossers, and between 10 percent and 15 percent actually have a college degree. Thus, they are spread more widely through the economy than popular wisdom suggests.

Moreover, employment verification through E-Verify is effective only against "on-the-books" employment. Such hiring is more likely to occur in higher-wage and higher-skill jobs and less likely to occur in low-wage fields such as construction and farm labor. This means that the "on-the-books" hiring of illegal immigrants is likely to be less concentrated in a few low-wage industries than is "off-the-books" hiring.

For these reasons, employment verification laws should apply to all industries equally to serve as a substantial deterrent to illegal immigration, and law enforcement actions should be prioritized to address the most egregious situations first.

> "[E-Verify] is a hugely flawed system and will have a severe effect on both naturalized U.S. citizens, as well as those who are native born."

Employment Verification Will Not Deter Illegal Immigration

Tom DeWeese

Tom DeWeese is president of the American Policy Center, a libertarian public policy and education organization. In the following viewpoint, DeWeese argues that the electronic employment verification system now in place for several businesses is flawed and dangerous. In DeWeese's view, the system is inaccurate, forces another burden on American businesses, and may increase fraud within the very system it was meant to rectify. In addition, DeWeese fears the E-Verify system will eventually be used to gather more personal identity information than needed to accomplish its mission, impinging on the privacy rights of American citizens.

Tom DeWeese, "E-Verify and the Emerging Surveillance State," NewsWithViews.com, September 29, 2008. http://www.newswithviews.com/DeWeese/tom119.htm. Reproduced by permission.

As you read, consider the following questions:

1. According to Jim Harper of the Cato Institute, what fraction of legal hires would immediately be found ineligible to work if the E-Verify system were imposed nationwide?

2. In DeWeese's opinion, how would E-Verify likely lead to more fraud in the employment identification system?

3. E-Verify sets the stage for what kind of government surveillance system, as DeWeese explains?

If government won't do its job, is that a reason for Americans to surrender their liberty? Do you think that is a funny question? Well, it is actually what a number of activist groups are now advocating in the name of stopping illegal immigration.

The fact is, the U.S. government is not doing its job to secure the border and stop the flood of illegal aliens from rushing across it. Even though Congress has passed legislation demanding that a fence be built, the Department of Homeland Security (DHS) is dragging its feet, holding up the project. Moreover, DHS is fighting efforts in local communities to allow police to arrest illegals. There is little effort to tighten visa security, or allow law enforcement to track down and deport those who stay here past their allotted time. Those illegals caught committing crimes are still allowed to leave, only to easily and surreptitiously return at their will. The border is a sieve. There is no border control—period.

Putting the Burden on Business

Rather than work to strengthen the borders and take steps to stop illegals from getting here in the first place, many now seek "internal enforcement" rather than the "rule of law." In other words, take action after leaving the barn door open.

The answer, say some very powerful anti-immigration forces, is to put the burden of control on American businesses. Jobs, they say, are the draw to illegals, so business should be the first line of defense. The answer, we are told, is simply to get tough with business and stop the ability of illegals to get a job. Such a plan, while appealing to desperate Americans, can have dire consequences if a nation desires to remain free.

Chief among the schemes to "get tough" with business is the universal enforcement of something called the E-Verify System. It is the brainchild of the Department of Homeland Security and is an electronic employment verification (EEV) program. Essentially, E-Verify uses the Social Security databases to verify Social Security Numbers to determine if someone is a U.S. citizen. Employers are to simply enter in the applicant's Social Security Number to verify they are an American citizen (of legal status) and therefore eligible for employment.

The Immigration Reform and Control Act of 1986 made it illegal for employers to "knowingly" employ unauthorized workers, and E-Verify (then known as "Basic Pilot") grew out of the requirement for work-eligibility verification. Since its inception the program has been voluntary for all businesses. However, that's about to change.

Selling the E-Verify System

In 2007, after the dramatic defeat of the illegal immigration amnesty bills, Homeland Security Secretary Michael Chertoff announced several changes to the E-Verify System. The agency will now require more than 200,000 federal contractors to use E-Verify, an increase of more than 1,076 percent over the 17,000 employers registered in 2007 (with only about half actually using) E-Verify. The system will use an "enhanced photograph capability" that will allow employers to check photographs in E-Verify databases. DHS will expand the number of databases E-Verify checks to include visa and passport databases, and the agency is asking states to "voluntarily" allow

pector General reported approximately 18 million of
cords are not accurate. Yet, DHS wants E-Verify made
ory for the entire American work force.

a matter of simple math," says Jim Harper at the CATO
e, "that means that if E-Verify were to go national, on
t day 1 in 25 legal hires would be bounced out of the
and asked to go down to the Social Security office and
ten out the problem."

agine the problems faced by honest, law abiding Ameri-
ho are thrown out of the system. In most cases, these
t well-to-do executives who can simply take the after-
off to fix the problem. They are lower level workers who
d on every dime they earn to pay the rent and feed the
imply taking a day off to go down to the local Social
ty office isn't an easy thing.

om the moment they are found to be a "tentative non-
med" they have eight days to contest the claim and to
they are legal. A day off work is required because the
Security office is only open from 8:30am to 5:00pm. If
mployer fails to make it to the office in the 8 days, the
oyer is required by threat of fine and criminal charges to
he employee.

mping Social Security Offices

eover, as the E-Verify system is forced on all employers
the large numbers of employees (as reported above) are
wn from the system, there will be a massive run on the
al Security office. The SS Administration is simply not
ipped to handle such a massive influx of cases. The infra-
cture to handle it is not in place.

As anyone who tried to get a passport last year knows,
en the government makes significant, mandatory changes
a system, typically government inefficiency rules. New rules
cerning passports forced Americans to flood passport of-
es, but the offices weren't prepared to receive and process

DHS access to their motor vehicle ⟨
employers to fire employees if they
match" discrepancies within 90 day:
terminate the workers' employment
fines of $11,000 or more. DHS also v
ployers by 25 percent and increasi
against employers, as opposed to adn

With those changes, E-Verify is
atom bomb in the war on illegal imm
as "the most effective tool to prote
workers from unscrupulous businesses
workers to displace American work
Sounds great—of course all of this co
System's ability to stop illegal immigr
FORE most businesses have even been

The fact is, there are major proble
System. It is a hugely flawed system and
fect on both naturalized U.S. citizens, as
native born.

Millions of Employees Could Mist
Fall Into Legal Limbo

Independent analyses of existing governi
found unacceptably high error rates. Curr
ily using E-Verify have experienced near
rates. Forcing more than 7 million employ
gal status of more than 160 million curren
as the millions of future hires, means that
as 17 million citizens and legal U.S. reside
enly found "ineligible" to work.

The fact is, the Social Security Administ
purges a Social Security number once it's as
dent database (which E-Verify uses) curre
million records; more than 100 million more
total population, legal or otherwise. In Dec

Electronic Verification Endangers Privacy

The EEV process would give [government agencies] access to a wealth of new data about every American's working situation. Because it uses the SSN [Social Security Number], EEV data would easily be correlated with tax records at the Internal Revenue Service, education loan records in the Department of Education, health records at the Department of Health and Human Services, and so on. Americans living with EEV should not expect that they could get work if they were in arrears on any debt to the U.S. government, for example.

Unless a clear, strong, and verifiable data destruction policy were in place, any EEV system, however benign in its inception, would be a surveillance system that tracked all American workers. The system would add to the data stores throughout the federal government that continually amass information about the lives, livelihoods, activities, and interests of everyone—especially law-abiding citizens.

Jim Harper,
"Electronic Employment Eligibility Verification:
Franz Kafka's Solution to Illegal Immigration,"
Policy Analysis *No. 612, Cato Institute, March 5, 2008.*

the massive number of applicants. The E-Verify System would force much larger numbers into unprepared Social Security offices.

Now, under E-Verify, employees that do make it to the SS office may be forced to return day after day. Jobs and income will be lost as the Employment Eligibility Verification (EEV) process does not permit employers to hold the jobs or delay start dates. The clock starts to tick the second the tentative non-confirmed notice is issued and runs out in exactly 8 days.

If it's all been a mistake, the burden of proof is on the employee to prove who they are and that they are legal citizens or residents eligible to continue working. These law-abiding American citizens enter the Social Security Office as criminal suspects with the potential of being deported. Contrary to American law, they are guilty until proven innocent. Incredibly, there is no appeals process in place to challenge the findings of E-Verify.

More Fraud—No Less

The E-Verify System is promoted as the only foolproof way to stop illegals from obtaining jobs. Advocates say the program has enough safeguards to protect citizens. Not so fast. Once the system is in place there are huge gaps that allow massive fraud.

To work efficiently, an E-Verify System allows employers access to a centralized record of all legal residents and citizens. Given the government's mixed record on data security, this could become a one-stop-shop for identity theft.

First, illegals and those employers wishing to hire them can simply work under the table, paying cash, hiding the transaction from any official source. Illegals don't regularly file income taxes, so the hire isn't hard to hide.

On a larger scale, it must be understood that illegal immigration is big business and it has the money and the means to create false documents and to provide "legal" identification, complete with matching names and Social Security numbers.

Today, many illegals simply make up names and Social Security numbers, hoping not to get caught. Of course, the E-Verify system would catch them. However, in response, an illegal only has to obtain the name and SS number of a legal citizen. While that legal person may already be working a job, it will not create an alert if the information is used by someone else.

Such information can be available through a wide variety of situations, including stolen lists and select employees with access to databases like the Social Security lists. Organized crime can certainly have well placed cohorts. The process would create a massive criminal market for Americans citizens' personal information.

The only way to stop it is for the federal government to create a new database that records every new hire and monitor all employees in the nation.

The real losers in this game are the people who have now had their identity stolen in the process. They may be the ones accused of identity theft as they suddenly discover someone else is using their name and SS number.

Poor Government Safeguards

Of course, the federal government has proven it has no ability to safeguard the records in its current databases. And the more databases established, the more opportunity for theft.

Recently, federal employees have been caught "sneaking a peek" at the passports of a large number of celebrities and even presidential candidates including Barack Obama, John McCain and Hillary Clinton.

In August of this year, the Transportation Security Administration (TSA) lost a laptop computer which contained the records of 33,000 people who had signed up for its prescreening program, designed to give travelers quicker access through airport security. The unencrypted information in the database included names, addresses, driver's license numbers, passport numbers, Social Security numbers, alien registration numbers, and current credit card numbers.

The laptop was in the possession of employees of a private company contracting with TSA for the project. TSA signup documents for the project promise that the records will be maintained at its headquarters in Arlington, VA, and "other authorized TSA or DHA secure facilities, as necessary, and at a digital safe site managed by a government contractor." In reality, the laptop was stashed in a locked office at the San Francisco Airport. There are a lot of laptops containing personal information of Americans being taken home by government employees these days. Why?

Mission Creep

The greatest threat from establishment of a system such as E-Verify is the creation of perhaps unintended results. As Cato's Jim Harper surmises, "The things to make a system like this impervious to forgery and fraud would convert it from an identity system into a cradle-to-grave biometric tracking system."

"Mission Creep" is the commonly used description for a program designed for a specific purpose, but is later used for much more. A prime example of mission creep is the Social Security System itself. It was designed specifically as a means for people to deposit money into a government program to provide for their retirement years. Today, there are those who want to take its databank of users and transform it into an identity system to prove American citizenship. "Well, it's already there!" That's mission creep.

As reported in the beginning, DHS Secretary Chertoff intends to increase the E-Verify system to include biometric photographs and extended databases. On numerous occasions Secretary Chertoff has expressed his desire to create a national identification card that would include near complete information on its bearer. This would include job, medical, tax, and school records. It would also include biometric and facial recognition, with RFID microchips that could monitor the whereabouts of every American.

E-Verify is the beginning of the creation of such a system. Is it worth it for Americans to endure an existence in a well-controlled matrix of surveillance simply to catch some illegal workers? Communities across the nation are proving that illegals will stop coming here—in fact actually leave—if they are made to feel unwelcome.

E-Verify sets the stage for a national workforce management system which gives the government ultimate power to decide who works and who doesn't. It is designed to ultimately subject all Americans to an intrusive global surveillance system as the information in DHS databanks is being transferred to international systems through such DHS partners as American Association of Motor Vehicle Administrators (AAMVA) and the International Civil Aviation Organization (ICAO).

The federal government has been given the mandate by the people to close the borders and keep them out. It doesn't require cradle-to-grave biometric tracking of every legal American to accomplish that task. Facts show that such "internal enforcement" would not reduce the illegality, it would promote it. Border security combined with real efforts by the government to keep illegals out of the country will do much more to stop the flood than chaining American citizens to massive, all knowing surveillance data banks.

"Immigration quotas forcibly exclude foreigners who want not to seize but to purchase housing here, who want not to rob Americans but to engage in productive work, raising our standard of living."

The United States Should Adopt Open Immigration

Harry Binswanger

Harry Binswanger, a professor of philosophy at the Ayn Rand Institute, states in the following viewpoint that America should adopt open immigration policies and dispense with the quota system. In Binswanger's view, people have the right freely to choose where they live and work; to limit or exclude immigrants therefore is an example of government overstepping its bounds and infringing on individual rights. Binswanger also dismisses notions that immigrants steal jobs from native workers, asserting instead that nations have limitless work to be done and that as long as immigrants are self-supporting, they should be welcomed into the labor pool to increase the amount of wealth countries can create.

As you read, consider the following questions:

1. In Binswanger's opinion, who should determine if an immigrant can live in a certain place or work at a certain job?

2. How does Binswanger undermine the "practical" arguments against immigration?

3. As Binswanger argues, what causes unemployment?

This is a defense of phasing-in open immigration into the United States. Entry into the U.S. should ultimately be free for any foreigner, with the exception of criminals, would-be terrorists, and those carrying infectious diseases. (And note: I am defending freedom of entry and residency, not the automatic granting of U.S. citizenship.)

An end to immigration quotas is demanded by the principle of individual rights. Every individual has rights as an individual, not as a member of this or that nation. One has rights not by virtue of being an American, but by virtue of being human.

One doesn't have to be a resident of any particular country to have a moral entitlement to be secure from governmental coercion against one's life, liberty, and property. In the words of the Declaration of Independence, government is instituted "to secure these rights"—to protect them against their violation by force or fraud.

A foreigner has rights just as much as an American. To be a foreigner is not to be a criminal. Yet our government treats as criminals those foreigners not lucky enough to win the green-card lottery.

Quotas Treat Immigrants as Criminals

Seeking employment in this country is not a criminal act. It coerces no one and violates no one's rights (there is no "right" to be exempt from competition in the labor market, or in any other market).

It is not a criminal act to buy or rent a home here in which to reside. Paying for housing is not a coercive act—whether the buyer is an American or a foreigner. No one's rights are violated when a Mexican, or Canadian, or Senegalese rents an apartment from an American owner and moves into the housing he is paying for. And what about the rights of those American citizens who want to sell or rent their property to the highest bidders? Or the American businesses that want to hire the lowest cost workers? It is morally indefensible for our government to violate their right to do so, just because the person is a foreigner.

Immigration quotas forcibly exclude foreigners who want not to seize but to purchase housing here, who want not to rob Americans but to engage in productive work, raising our standard of living. To forcibly exclude those who seek peacefully to trade value for value with us is a violation of the rights of both parties to such a trade: the rights of the American seller or employer and the rights of the foreign buyer or employee.

Thus, immigration quotas treat both Americans and foreigners as if they were criminals, as if the peaceful exchange of values to mutual benefit were an act of destruction.

The Rights of the Individual Above All

To take an actual example, if I want to invite my Norwegian friend Klaus to live in my home, either as a guest or as a paying tenant, what right does our government have to stop Klaus and me? To be a Norwegian is not to be a criminal. And if some American business wants to hire Klaus, what right does our government have to interfere?

The implicit premise of barring foreigners is: "This is our country, we let in who we want." But who is "we"? The government does not own the country. Jurisdiction is not ownership. Only the owner of land or any item of property can decide the terms of its use or sale. Nor does the majority own the country. This is a country of private property, and housing is private property. So is a job.

American land is not the collective property of some entity called "the U.S. government." Nor is there such thing as collective, social ownership of the land. The claim, "We have the right to decide who is allowed in" means some individuals—those with the most votes—claim the right to prevent other citizens from exercising their rights. But there can be no right to violate the rights of others.

Our constitutional republic respects minority rights. 60% of the population cannot vote to enslave the other 40%. Nor can a majority dictate to the owners of private property. Nor can a majority dictate on whom private employers spend their money. Not morally, not in a free society. In a free society, the rights of the individual are held sacrosanct, above any claim of even an overwhelming majority.

The rights of one man end where the rights of his neighbor begin. Only within the limits of his rights is a man free to act on his own judgment. The criminal is the man who deliberately steps outside his rights-protected domain and invades the domain of another, depriving his victim of his exclusive control over his property, or liberty, or life. The criminal, by his own choice, has rejected rights in favor of brute violence. Thus, an immigration policy that excludes criminals is proper.

Likewise, a person with an infectious disease, such as smallpox, threatens with serious physical harm those with whom he comes into proximity. Unlike the criminal, he may not intend to do damage, but the threat of physical harm is clear, present, and objectively demonstrable. To protect the lives of Americans, he may be kept out or quarantined until he is no longer a threat.

But what about the millions of Mexicans, South Americans, Chinese, Canadians, etc. seeking entry who are not criminal and not bearing infectious diseases? By what moral principle can they be excluded? Not on the grounds of majority

The Market Supports Immigrants

Every day we see the willingness of Americans to accommodate immigrants. The market supports them. They work, purchase goods and services, and pay for housing. Their use of public resources and land, if anything, is a problem with the status of so much property as public—just as their potential abuse of welfare is a problem with welfare itself. Continuing to shut out immigrants, or becoming even more restrictive with the borders, further reinforces the notion that so much public land should be protected by government, and takes us a step away from our ultimate goal of eventually privatizing it. Once most land is privatized, most immigrants would be able to find work and housing in the marketplace, and in the meantime the government cannot mimic the proper supply and demand for labor in lieu of market mechanisms.

Anthony Gregory,
"In Defense of Open Immigration,"
Freedom Daily, *October 2004.*

vote, not on the grounds of protecting any American's rights, not on the grounds of any legitimate authority of the state.

Understanding the Nature of Rights

That's the moral case for phasing out limits on immigration. But some ask: "Is it practical? Wouldn't unlimited immigration—even if phased in over a decade—be disastrous to our economic well-being and create overcrowding? Are we being told to just grit our teeth and surrender our interests in the name of morality?"

This question is invalid on its face. It shows a failure to understand the nature of rights, and of moral principles generally. Rational moral principles reflect a recognition of the basic nature of man, his nature as a specific kind of living organism, having a specific means of survival. Questions of what is practical, what is to one's self-interest, can be answered only in that context. It is neither practical nor to one's interest to attempt to live and act in defiance of one's nature as a human being.

Yet that is the meaning of the moral-practical dichotomy. When one claims, "It is immoral but practical," one is maintaining, "It cripples my nature as a human being, but it is beneficial to me"—which is a contradiction.

Rights, in particular, are not something pulled from the sky or decreed by societal whim. Rights are moral principles, established by reference to the needs inherent in man's nature qua man. "Rights are conditions of existence required by man's nature for his proper survival." ([philosopher and author] Ayn Rand)

Every organism has a basic means of survival; for man, that means is: reason. Man is the rational animal, *homo sapiens*. Rights are moral principles that spell out the terms of social interaction required for a rational being to survive and flourish. Since the reasoning mind cannot function under physical coercion, the basic social requirement of man's survival is: freedom. Rights prescribe freedom by proscribing coercion.

"If man is to live on earth, it is right for him to use his mind, it is right to act on his own free judgment, it is right to work for his values and to keep the product of his work." (Ayn Rand)

Rights reflect the fundamental alternative of voluntary consent or brute force. The reign of force is in no one's interest; the system of voluntary cooperation by mutual consent is the precondition of anyone achieving his actual interests....

Work Is Limitless

One major fear of open immigration is economic: the fear of losing one's job to immigrants. It is asked: "Won't the immigrants take our jobs?" The answer is: "Yes, so we can go on to better, higher-paying jobs."

The fallacy in this protectionist objection lies in the idea that there is only a finite amount of work to be done. The unstated assumption is: "If Americans don't get to do that work, if foreigners do it instead, we Americans will have nothing to do."

But work is the creation of wealth. A job is a role in the production of goods and services—the production of food, of cars, computers, the providing of internet content—all the items that go to make up our standard of living. A country cannot have too much wealth. The need for wealth is limitless, and the work that is to be done is limitless. . . .

Unemployment is not caused by an absence of avenues for the creation of wealth. Unemployment is caused by government interference in the labor market. Even with that interference, the number of jobs goes relentlessly upward, decade after decade. This bears witness to the fact that there's no end to the creation of wealth and thus no end to the useful employment of human intelligence and the physical effort directed by that intelligence. There is always more productive work to be done. If you can give your job to an immigrant, you can get a more valuable job.

What is the effect of a bigger labor pool on wage rates? If the money supply is constant, nominal wage rates fall. But real wage rates rise because total output has gone up. Economists have demonstrated that real wages have to rise as long as the immigrants are self-supporting. If immigrants earn their keep, if they don't consume more than they produce, then they add to total output, which means that prices fall (if the money supply is constant).

And, in fact, rising real wages was the history of our country in the nineteenth century. Before the 1920s, there were no limits on immigration, yet our standard of living rocketed upward. Self-supporting immigrants were an economic benefit not an injury.

The protectionist objection that immigrants take away jobs and harm our standard of living is a solid economic fallacy.

Welfare and Overcrowding Concerns

A popular misconception is that immigrants come here to get welfare. To the extent that is true, immigrants do constitute a burden. But this issue is mooted by the passage, under the [Bill] Clinton Administration, of the Personal Responsibility and Work Opportunity and Reconciliation Act (PRWORA), which makes legal permanent residents ineligible for most forms of welfare for 5 years. I support this kind of legislation.

Further, if the fear is of non-working immigrants, why is the pending legislation aimed at employers of immigrants?

America is a vastly underpopulated country. Our population density is less than one-third of France's.

Take an extreme example. Suppose a tidal wave of immigrants came here. Suppose that half of the people on the planet moved here. That would mean an unthinkable elevenfold increase in our population—from 300 million to 3.3 billion people. That would make America almost as "densely" populated as today's England (360 people/sq. km. vs. 384 people/sq. km.). In fact, it would make us less densely populated than the state of New Jersey (453 per sq. km.). And these calculations exclude Alaska and Hawaii, and count only land area.

Contrary to widespread beliefs, high population density is a value not a disvalue. High population density intensifies the division of labor, which makes possible a wider variety of jobs and specialized consumer products. For instance, in Manhattan, there is a "doll hospital"—a store specializing in the repair of children's dolls. Such a specialized, niche business requires a high population density in order to have a market. Try finding a doll hospital in Poughkeepsie. In Manhattan, one can find a job as a Pilates Method teacher or as a "Secret Shopper" (two jobs actually listed on Craig's List [www.craigslist.org]). Not in Paducah.

People want to live near other people, in cities. One-seventh of England's population lives in London. If population density is a bad thing, why are Manhattan real-estate prices so high?

The Value of Immigrants

Immigrants are the kind of people who refresh the American spirit. They are ambitious, courageous, and value freedom. They come here, often with no money and not even speaking the language, to seek a better life for themselves and their children.

The vision of American freedom, with its opportunity to prosper by hard work, serves as a magnet drawing the best of the world's people. Immigrants are self-selected for their virtues: their ambitiousness, daring, independence, and pride. They are willing to cast aside the tradition-bound roles assigned to them in their native lands and to re-define themselves as Americans. These are the people America needs in order to keep alive the individualist, hard-working attitude that made America.

Here is a short list of some great immigrants: Alexander Hamilton, Alexander Graham Bell, Andrew Carnegie, most of the top scientists of the Manhattan Project, Igor Sikorsky (the inventor of the helicopter), Ayn Rand.

Open immigration: the benefits are great. The right is unquestionable. So let them come.

> "I submit that 'immigration control' is
> perfectly Libertarian, a necessary ex-
> tension of the 'right not to associate.'"

The United States Should Not Adopt Open Immigration

Vin Suprynowicz

In the viewpoint that follows, Vin Suprynowicz contends that open immigration should not be a libertarian ideal. In Suprynowicz's view, allowing all immigrants to enter or remain in America would lead to overcrowding, poverty, and increased taxes. He also fears that allowing in so many immigrants would give them the political power to run the country by majority vote and subsequently trample the rights of individuals. Vin Suprynowicz is the assistant editorial page editor for the Las Vegas Review-Journal.

As you read, consider the following questions:

1. Why does Suprynowicz oppose giving amnesty to illegal immigrants already in the United States?
2. What libertarian "right" does the author equate with immigration control?

3. What laws does Suprynowicz suggest "socialist Californians" might impose on the hypothetical New Columbia
libertarian experiment if majority rule came into effect?

The May 24 headline announced "Marchers want legality
for undocumented teens."

A few dozen local college kids were out to express their
outrage that another amnesty for illegal aliens (the last one
was in 1986)—a "DREAM [Development, Relief and Education for Alien Minors] Act" that would have allowed illegals
brought to this country by their parents when they were 15 or
younger to "move toward legality"—failed in the U.S. Senate
last year, 52–44, after voters got wind of what they were up to.

The marchers say they want these anchor babies to be
given a "path to legal status." They've already got one: Go
back to your U.S. embassy or consulate in Mexico or Guatemala or El Salvador and fill out your Immigration forms and
wait your turn.

What those who prefer the simpering euphemism "undocumented" really want is not "reform" but amnesty—for
the laws violated by these invaders to be treated as though
they never existed.

The question they don't want to answer is how they would
compensate all the doctors and artisans and chemical engineers—many of them literate and fluent in English—who
have been patiently waiting their turn in the U.S. immigration
line in Bosnia and Belarus and Burundi, in India and Iran and
Thailand and Tasmania. Their places in line—usurped without compensation—surely have cash value. Why should we be
complicit in the theft of their dreams?

"They're here!" the scofflaws shout. "You have to acknowledge reality! You can't round up and deport millions of
people!"

Wow. Should we have told the French in 1943, "There's
nothing we can do; the undocumented Guest Germans are al-

ready there!"? What if instead of fighting the battle of Edington, King Alfred had told the Britons "We can't round up all these Danes and deport them! Live with the reality; learn to speak Danish; the undocumented GuestDanes are already here!"?

Libertarians often chide me for taking a position other than the supposed "proper" Libertarian position on immigration, which (they assert) calls for open borders and no restrictions on the movement of peoples, whatever.

I believe they're wrong.

Have these gentle souls never seen the barrios that spring up on the hillsides outside many a Central and South American city—thousands of people living in cardboard packing crates and hovels made of old plastic sheeting, drawing water from a polluted common well, raw sewage flowing down the middle of the "streets"? Would they like a few million such souls to start trooping into this country and setting up shop outside New York, Philadelphia, Phoenix, San Diego and Baton Rouge? What will our reliable liberals then demand? That we build these people proper public housing, of course, with indoor hot and cold running water, central heat and air conditioning, color televisions, all at taxpayer expense.

Are you nuts?

I submit that "immigration control" is perfectly Libertarian, a necessary extension of the "right not to associate." It starts with the gang of hoboes showing up at your front door, demanding to move in with you and decide "by majority vote" who gets to eat all the food out of your refrigerator. You have the right—the duty to your family, unless you're nuts—to turn them away. So why can't you delegate that power?

Imagine with me that a few hundred Libertarians, happening across a couple of billionaires who see things our way, were allowed to establish a free Republic of New Columbia by

America Does Not Need a Low-Wage Economy

It is true, of course, that the existence of a large and growing supply of unskilled workers tends to reduce prices—especially the price of lawn mowing, Tyson's chicken, and certain kinds of fruits and vegetables. But if you think that the more unskilled laborers we have, the larger and more dynamic the economy will be, you have a strange idea about the production of wealth. When I have my car washed, some of the work is done by unskilled labor, but as much as possible is done by machines. If more human squirters and swabbers were available, I'm sure that the price of their labor would go down, and at some point the machines would be completely replaced by muscles. The same might be said about, say, the sweeping of streets or the growing of crops. I don't believe, however, that a low-wage, labor-intensive economy is preferable in any way to a machine economy, paying high wages to well-educated people. If you believe that, you belong in the pre-industrial age. . . .

[Some people] think that wealth results automatically from toil. It doesn't. And great increases in wealth never do. They result from the kind of work that is done by people who are highly skilled and, ordinarily, highly paid. Our immigration policy should target the entrepreneurs, the professionals, the wealth producers, and make it easy for them to come to America—supposing, as I do, that doctors and software engineers do something more for the economy than the guys behind the counter of the local 7–11.

Stephen Cox, *"The Fallacy of Open Immigration,"*
Liberty, October 2006.

buying half a county somewhere on the Pacific coast of Oregon. (The statists-in-charge will never allow this, but let's pretend.)

We send constructive notice to all the former county, state and federal authorities that we've declared our independence, that we have no need of their "services" and will not be sending them any tax payments.

In short order, a bunch of Southern Californians spot us and say, "Hey, if we move up there we won't have to pay all these darn taxes!" Pretty soon a few thousand of them are squatting on our land, living in RVs and tents. And what do they do? Within months they express shock that they're expected to pay cash to use the private streets, cash for their medical care and the tutoring of their children—no more "tax-paid benefits"!

They promptly demand a big election, at which they plan to "decide by majority vote" to pass bond issues to build "public schools," to ban the private possession of firearms, to mandate recycling, to ban charcoal grills in order to save the polar bear, to replace our private schools and volunteer fire department with unionized, tax-paid "professionals" funded with "progressive taxes on the wealthy," etc.

How long would your Libertarian experiment last? And this isn't just a theory. It's already happened to once-mostly-Libertarian Nevada. We call it "Californication."

To keep from becoming a colony of socialist California, you'd have no choice but to meet new arrivals at the border, telling them they're welcome to pass through New Columbia as tourists for a few days so long as they pay their private road tolls (no taxes, remember), but they can't stay and settle down unless they sign a compact agreeing never to demand any "majority votes" on the presumption that such a method can legitimately authorize taxes, regulations, etc.

What would you call such border posts, where new arrivals are greeted? No matter what you called them, what they'd be up to would be "immigration control," which would be absolutely necessary if you didn't want to lose your freedoms to a "majority vote" of invading socialists, within the first year.

Border control—at your front door, or along Interstate 19 from Nogales. So long as there are collectivists anxious and able to infiltrate our ranks and subvert our rights under the guise of "one-man, one-vote democracy" . . . there can be no freedom without it.

"If our immigration system is so lax that it can be penetrated by a Mexican busboy, it can sure be penetrated by an Al-Qaeda terrorist."

Lax Immigration Policies Invite Terrorism

Mark Krikorian

In the following viewpoint, Mark Krikorian maintains that America has lax immigration policies that allow terrorists as well as illegal aliens easily to take up residence in the country. In Krikorian's view, the United States already has immigration deterrents in place, but many need improvement; he also believes that these countermeasures are not functioning properly because too many policymakers favor a more open immigration system and therefore have no interest in strengthening those defenses. Krikorian insists that America adhere to strict immigration law enforcement to avoid another terrorist attack. Mark Krikorian is the director of the Center for Immigration Studies, a think tank that advocates tighter immigration controls.

Mark Krikorian, "Keeping Terror Out: Immigration Policy and Asymmetric Warfare," *The National Interest*, Spring 2004, pp. 77–85. Copyright © 2004 The National Interest, Washington, DC. Reproduced by permission.

As you read, consider the following questions:

1. As Krikorian states, what were the characteristics of the 9/11 terrorists that should have flagged them as the kinds of people that are likely to overstay their visas?
2. What improvements has the government made to the visa program, according to Krikorian?
3. What are city "sanctuary" policies and why does Krikorian find them problematic?

Supporters of open immigration have tried to de-link 9/11 from security concerns. "There's no relationship between immigration and terrorism", said a spokeswoman for the National Council of the advocacy group La Raza. "I don't think [9/11] can be attributed to the failure of our immigration laws," claimed the head of the immigration lawyers' guild a week after the attacks.

President [George W.] Bush has not gone that far, but in his January 7 [2004] speech proposing an illegal alien amnesty and guest worker program, he claimed the federal government is now fulfilling its responsibility to control immigration, thus justifying a vast increase in the flow of newcomers to America. Exploring the role of immigration control in promoting American security can help provide the context to judge the president's claim that his proposal is consistent with our security imperatives, and can help to sketch the outlines of a secure immigration system.

The New Home Front

The phrase "Home Front" is a metaphor that gained currency during World War I with the intention of motivating a civilian population involved in total war. The image served to increase economic output and the purchase of war bonds, promote conservation and the recycling of resources and reconcile the citizenry to privation and rationing.

But in the wake of 9/11, "Home Front" is no longer a metaphor. As Deputy Secretary of Defense Paul Wolfowitz said in October 2002,

> Fifty years ago, when we said, 'home front,' we were referring to citizens back home doing their part to support the war front. Since last September, however, the home front has become a battlefront every bit as real as any we've known before.

Nor is this an aberration unique to Al-Qaeda or to Islamists generally. No enemy has any hope of defeating our armies in the field and must therefore resort to asymmetric means. And though there are many facets to asymmetric or "Fourth-Generation" warfare—as we saw in Al-Qaeda's pre-9/11 assaults on our interests in the Middle East and East Africa and as we are seeing today in Iraq. The Holy Grail of such a strategy is mass-casualty attacks on America. . . .

Because of the asymmetric nature of the threat, the burden of homeland defense is not borne mainly by our armed forces but by agencies formerly seen as civilian entities—mainly the Department of Homeland Security (DHS). And of DHS's expansive portfolio, immigration control is central. The reason is elementary: no matter the weapon or delivery system—hijacked airliners, shipping containers, suitcase nukes, anthrax spores—operatives are required to carry out the attacks. Those operatives have to enter and work in the United States. In a very real sense, the primary weapons of our enemies are not inanimate objects at all, but rather the terrorists themselves—especially in the case of suicide attackers. Thus, keeping the terrorists out or apprehending them after they get in is indispensable to victory. As President Bush said recently, "Our country is a battlefield in the first war of the 21st century."

The Terrorists Are Here

In the words of the July 2002 National Strategy for Homeland Security:

> Our great power leaves these enemies with few conventional options for doing us harm. One such option is to take advantage of our freedom and openness by secretly inserting terrorists into our country to attack our homeland. Homeland security seeks to deny this avenue of attack to our enemies and thus to provide a secure foundation for America's ongoing global engagement.

Our enemies have repeatedly exercised this option of inserting terrorists by exploiting weaknesses in our immigration system. A [2002] Center for Immigration Studies analysis of the immigration histories of the 48 foreign-born Al-Qaeda operatives who committed crimes in the United States from 1993 to 2001 (including the 9/11 hijackers) found that nearly every element of the immigration system has been penetrated by the enemy. Of the 48, one-third were here on various temporary visas, another third were legal residents or naturalized citizens, one-fourth were illegal aliens, and the remainder had pending asylum applications. Nearly half of the total had, at some point or another, violated existing immigration laws.

Supporters of loose borders deny that inadequate immigration control is a problem, usually pointing to flawed intelligence as the most important shortcoming that needs to be addressed. Mary Ryan, for example, former head of the State Department's Bureau of Consular Affairs (which issues visas), testified in January 2004 before the 9/11 Commission that

> Even under the best immigration controls, most of the September 11 terrorists would still be admitted to the United States today ... because they had no criminal records, or known terrorist connections, and had not been identified by intelligence methods for special scrutiny.

The Terrorists Should Have Been Kept Out

But this turns out to be untrue, both for the hijackers and for earlier Al-Qaeda operatives in the United States. A normal level of visa scrutiny, for instance, would have excluded almost all the hijackers. Investigative reporter Joel Mowbray acquired copies of 15 of the 19 hijackers' visa applications (the other four were destroyed—yes, destroyed—by the State Department), and every one of the half-dozen current and former consular officers he consulted said every application should have been rejected on its face. Every application was incomplete or contained patently inadequate or absurd answers.

Even if the application had been properly prepared, many of the hijackers, including Mohammed Atta and several others, were young, single and had little income—precisely the kind of person likely to overstay his visa and become an illegal alien, and thus the kind of applicant who should be rejected. And, conveniently, those *least* likely to overstay their visas—older people with close family, property and other commitments in their home countries—are also the very people least likely to commit suicide attacks.

9/11 was not the only terrorist plot to benefit from lax enforcement of ordinary immigration controls—every major Al-Qaeda attack or conspiracy in the United States has involved at least one terrorist who violated immigration law. Gazi Ibrahim Abu Mezer, for example, who was part of the plot to bomb the Brooklyn subway, was actually caught three times by the Border Patrol trying to sneak in from Canada. The third time the Canadians would not take him back. What did we do? Because of a lack of detention space, he was simply released into the country and told to show up for his deportation hearing. After all, with so many millions of illegal aliens here already, how much harm could one more do?

Another example is Mohammed Salameh, who rented the truck in the first World Trade Center bombing. He should never have been granted a visa in the first place. When he applied for a tourist visa he was young, single and had no income and, in the event, did indeed end up remaining illegally. And when his application for a green card under the 1986 illegal-alien amnesty was rejected, there was (and remains today) no way to detain and remove rejected green card applicants, so he simply remained living and working in the United States, none the worse for wear. . . .

Ordinary immigration enforcement actually *has* kept out several terrorists that we know of. A vigilant inspector in Washington state stopped Ahmed Ressam because of nervous behavior, and a search of his car uncovered a trunk full of explosives, apparently intended for an attack on Los Angeles International Airport. Ramzi Binalshibh, one of the candidates for the label of "20th hijacker," was rejected four times for a visa, not because of concerns about terrorism but rather, according to a U.S. embassy source, "for the most ordinary of reasons, the same reasons most people are refused." That is, he was thought likely to overstay his visa and become an illegal alien. And Mohamed Al-Qahtani, another one of the "20th hijacker" candidates, was turned away by an airport inspector in Orlando because he had no return ticket and no hotel reservations, and he refused to identify the friend who was supposed to help him on his trip.

Prior to the growth of militant Islam, the only foreign threat to our population and territory in recent history has been the specter of nuclear attack by the Soviet Union. To continue that analogy, since the terrorists are themselves the weapons, immigration control is to asymmetric warfare what missile defense is to strategic warfare. There are other weapons we must use against an enemy employing asymmetric means—more effective international coordination, improved intelligence gathering and distribution, special military operations—but in the end, the lack of effective immigration control leaves us naked in the face of the enemy. This lack of defensive capability may have made sense with regard to the strategic nuclear threat under the doctrine of Mutual Assured Destruction, but it makes no sense with regard to the asymmetric threats we face today and in the future. . . .

Homeland Security Begins Abroad

To extend the missile defense analogy, there are three layers of immigration control, comparable to the three phases of a ballistic missile's flight: boost, midcourse and terminal. In immigration the layers are overseas, at the borders and inside the country. But unlike existing missile defense systems, the redundancy built into our immigration control system permits us repeated opportunities to exclude or apprehend enemy operatives.

Entry into America by foreigners is not a right but a privilege, granted exclusively at the discretion of the American people. The first agency that exercises that discretion is the State Department's Bureau of Consular Affairs, whose officers make the all-important decisions about who gets a visa. Consular Affairs is, in effect, America's other Border Patrol. In September 2003, DHS Under Secretary Asa Hutchinson described the visa process as "forward-based defense" against terrorists and criminals.

The visa filter is especially important because the closer an alien comes to the United States the more difficult it is to exclude him. There is relatively little problem, practically or politically, in rejecting a foreign visa applicant living abroad. Once a person presents himself at a port of entry, it becomes more difficult to turn him back, although the immigration inspector theoretically has a free hand to do so. Most difficult of all is finding and removing people who have actually been admitted; not only is there no physical chokepoint where aliens can be controlled, but even the most superficial connections with American citizens or institutions can lead to vocal protests against enforcement of the law.

Even before 9/11, some improvements had been made to the first layer of immigration security; visas were made machine-readable and more difficult to forge than in the past, and the "watch list" of people who should not be granted visas was computerized, replacing the old microfiche-based system in place until just a few years ago.

Since the attacks, further improvements have taken place. The State Department has instituted the Biometric Visa Program at several consular posts and is preparing to meet a statutory deadline later [in 2004] for all visas to have biometric data, in the form of fingerprints and photographs. What's more, under a memorandum of understanding signed last fall, DHS assumed oversight and veto authority over the issuance of visas, and now has personnel overseeing visa officers in a number of consular posts overseas, including in Saudi Arabia, Egypt, Indonesia, Morocco, Pakistan and the UAE [United Arab Emirates]. . . .

Order at the Border

The next layer of immigration security is the border, which has two elements: "ports of entry", which are the points where people traveling by land, sea or air enter the United States; and the stretches between those entry points. The first are staffed by inspectors working for DHS's Bureau of Customs and Border Protection, the second monitored by the Border Patrol and the Coast Guard, both now also part of DHS.

This is another important chokepoint, as almost all of the 48 Al-Qaeda operatives who committed terrorist acts through 2001 had had contact with immigration inspectors. But here, too, the system failed to do its job. For instance, Mohammed Atta was permitted to reenter the country in January 2001 even though he had overstayed his visa the last time. Also, before 9/11 hijacker Khalid Al-Midhar's second trip to the United States, the CIA learned that he had been involved in the bombing of the U.S.S. *Cole*—but it took months for his name to be

Border Control Must Be a Weapon in the National Security Arsenal

Despite [the] knowledge of illegal immigration and terrorist movement, more than half a million people about whom American law enforcement knows little or nothing will enter and remain in the United States in 2007. The overwhelming number of these people are those seeking nothing more than a job and a paycheck. It is within the background of these immigrants that terrorists lurk. The urgency to secure America's borders, and consequently its interior, from agents of terror could not be greater and requires no justification beyond American sovereignty. Falling towers in New York and a burning Pentagon in Washington describe better than words the need for heightened vigilance and enforcement at American ports and borders. Yet in August 2004, three years after the attacks, 9/11 Commission staff wrote:

> It is perhaps obvious to state that terrorists cannot plan and carry out attacks in the United States if they are unable to enter the country. Yet prior to September 11th . . . no agency of the U.S. government thought of border security as a tool in the counterterrorism arsenal. Indeed, even after 19 hijackers demonstrated the relative ease of obtaining a U.S. visa and gaining admission into the United States, border security still is not considered a cornerstone of national security.

Immigration, secure borders, and terrorism are linked, not because all immigrants are terrorists, but because nearly all terrorists in the West have been immigrants.

Cato,
"Coming to America: The Weaponization of Immigration,"
Washburn Law Journal, *Winter 2007.*

placed on the watch list used by airport inspectors, and by then he had already entered the country. And in any case, there still are twelve separate watch lists, maintained by nine different government agencies.

Political considerations fostered a dangerous culture of permissiveness in airport inspections. Bowing to complaints from airlines and the travel industry, Congress in 1990 required that incoming planes be cleared within 45 minutes, reinforcing the notion that the border was a nuisance to be evaded rather than a vital security tool. And the Orlando immigration inspector who turned back a Saudi national—Al-Qahtani, now believed to have been a part of the 9/11 plot—was well aware that he was taking a career risk, since Saudis were supposed to be treated even more permissively than other foreign nationals seeking entry.

There were also failures *between* the ports of entry. Abdelghani Meskini and Abdel Hakim Tizegha, both part of the Millennium Plot that included Ahmed Ressam, first entered the country as stowaways on ships that docked at U.S. ports. Tizegha later moved to Canada and then returned to the United States by sneaking across the land border. And of course, Abu Mezer, though successfully apprehended by the U.S. Border Patrol, was later released.

And finally, perhaps the biggest defect in this layer of security is the lack of effective tracking of departures. Without exit controls, there is no way to know who has overstayed his visa. This is especially important because most illegal alien terrorists have been overstayers. The opportunities for failure are numerous and the system is so dysfunctional that the INS's own statistics division declared that it was no longer possible to estimate the number of people who have overstayed their visas.

Certainly, there have been real improvements since 9/11. The US-VISIT system has begun to be implemented, with arriving visa-holders being digitally photographed and having their index fingerprints scanned: this will eventually grow into a "check in/check out" system to track them and other foreign visitors. Also, the 45-minute maximum for clearing foreign travelers has been repealed. Lastly, all foreign carriers are now required to forward their passenger manifests to immigration before the plane arrives. . . .

Safety Through Redundancy

The third layer of immigration security—the terminal phase, in missile defense jargon—is interior enforcement. Here, again, ordinary immigration control can be a powerful security tool. Of the 48 Al-Qaeda operatives, nearly half were either illegal aliens at the time of their crimes or had violated immigration laws at some point prior to their terrorist acts.

Many of these terrorists lived, worked, opened bank accounts and received driver's licenses with little or no difficulty. Because such a large percentage of terrorists violated immigration laws, enforcing the law would be extremely helpful in disrupting and preventing terrorist attacks.

But interior enforcement is also the most politically difficult part of immigration control. While there is at least nominal agreement on the need for improvements to the mechanics of visas and border monitoring, there is no elite consensus regarding interior enforcement. This is especially dangerous given that interior enforcement is the last rollback for immigration control, the final link in a chain of redundancy that starts with the visa application overseas.

There are two elements to interior enforcement: first, conventional measures such as arrest, detention and deportation; and second, verification of legal status when conducting important activities. The latter element is important because its goal is to disrupt the lives of illegal aliens so that many will return home on their own (and, in a security context, to disrupt the planning and execution of terrorist attacks).

Inadequacies in the first element of interior enforcement have clearly helped terrorists in the past. Because there is no way of determining which visitors have overstayed their visas, much less a mechanism for apprehending them, this has been a common means of remaining in the United States—of the twelve (out of 48) Al-Qaeda operatives who were illegal aliens when they took part in terrorism, seven were visa overstayers.

Among terrorists who were actually detained for one reason or another, several were released to go about their business inside America because of inadequate detention space. This lack of space means that most aliens in deportation proceedings are not detained, so that when ordered deported, they receive what is commonly known as a "run letter" instructing them to appear for deportation—and 94 percent of aliens from terrorist-sponsoring states disappear instead.

Lack of coordination between state and local police and federal immigration authorities is another major shortcoming. In the normal course of their work, police frequently encounter aliens. For instance, Mohammed Atta was ticketed in Broward County, Florida, in the spring of 2001 for driving without a license. But the officer had no mechanism to inform him that Atta had overstayed his visa during his prior trip to the United States. Although not an overstayer, another hijacker, Ziad Samir Jarrah, was issued a speeding ticket in Maryland just two days before 9/11, proving that even the most effective terrorists have run afoul of the law before launching their attacks.

Flawed Chokepoints

Perhaps the most outrageous phenomenon in this area of conventional immigration enforcement is the adoption of "sanctuary" policies by cities across the country. Such policies prohibit city employees—including police—from reporting immigration violations to federal authorities or even inquiring as to a suspect's immigration status. It is unknown whether any terrorists have yet eluded detention with the help of such policies, but there is no doubt that many ordinary murderers, drug dealers, gang members and other undesirables have and will continue to do so.

The second element of interior enforcement has been, if anything, even more neglected. The creation of "virtual chokepoints", where an alien's legal status would be verified, is an important tool of immigration control, making it difficult for illegals to engage in the activities necessary for modern life.

The most important chokepoint is employment. Unfortunately, enforcement of the prohibition against hiring illegal aliens, passed in 1986, has all but stopped. This might seem to be of little importance to security, but in fact holding a job can be important to terrorists for a number of reasons. By giving them a means of support, it helps them blend into society. Neighbors might well become suspicious of young men who do not work but seem able to pay their bills. Moreover, supporting themselves by working would enable terrorists to avoid the scrutiny that might attend the transfer of money from abroad. Of course, terrorists who do not work can still arrive with large sums of cash, but this too creates risks of detection.

That said, the ban on employment by illegal aliens is one of the most widely violated immigration laws by terrorists. Among those who worked illegally at some point were CIA shooter Mir Aimal Kansi: Millennium plot conspirator Abdelghani Meskini; and 1993 World Trade Center bombers Eyad Ismoil, Mohammed Salameh and Mahmed and Mohammed Abouhalima.

Other chokepoints include obtaining a driver's license and opening a bank account, two things that most of the 9/11 hijackers had done. It is distressing to note that, while Virginia, Florida and New Jersey tightened their driver's license rules after learning that the hijackers had used licenses from those states, other states have not. Indeed, California's then-

Governor Gray Davis signed a bill last year [2003] intended specifically to provide licenses to illegal aliens (which was repealed after his recall). . . .

Finally, the provision of immigration services is an important chokepoint, one that provides the federal government additional opportunities to screen the same alien. There is a hierarchy of statuses a foreign-born person might possess, from illegal alien to short-term visitor, long-term visitor, permanent resident (green card holder) and finally, naturalized citizen. It is very beneficial for terrorists to move up in this hierarchy because it affords them additional opportunities to harm us. To take only one example: Mahmud Abouhalima—one of the leaders of the first World Trade Center bombing—was an illegal-alien visa overstayer; but he became a legal resident as part of the 1986 illegal-alien amnesty by falsely claiming to be a farm worker, and he was only then able to travel to Afghanistan for terrorist training and return to the United States. . . .

Upholding the Law

Such ambivalence about immigration enforcement, at whatever stage in the process, compromises our security. It is important to understand that the security function of immigration control is not merely opportunistic, like prosecuting Al Capone for tax violations for want of evidence on his other numerous crimes. The FBI's use of immigration charges to detain hundreds of Middle Easterners in the immediate aftermath of 9/11 was undoubtedly necessary, but it cannot be a model for the role of immigration law in homeland security. If our immigration system is so lax that it can be penetrated by a Mexican busboy, it can sure be penetrated by an Al-Qaeda terrorist.

Since there is no way to let in "good" illegal aliens but keep out "bad" ones, countering the asymmetric threats to our people and territory requires sustained, across-the-board immigration law enforcement. Anything less exposes us to grave dangers. Whatever the arguments for the president's amnesty and guest worker plan, no such proposal can plausibly be entertained until we have a robust, functioning immigration-control system. And we are nowhere close to that day.

Periodical Bibliography

The following articles have been selected to supplement the diverse views presented in this chapter.

Jeff Faux	"What to Really Do About Immigration," *American Prospect*, January-February 2008.
David Frum	"How I Rethought Immigration," *National Review*, June 25, 2007.
Daniel Gross et al.	"The New Dream Isn't American," *Newsweek*, May 26, 2008.
Gordon H. Hanson	"Free Markets Need Free People," *Wall Street Journal*, April 10, 2007.
John B. Judis	"Phantom Menace," *New Republic*, Febrary 13, 2008.
John F. Kavanaugh	"Amnesty?" *America*, March 10, 2008.
Mike Kraus	"A Way Out of the Immigration Mess," *Wall Street Journal*, July 21, 2007.
Michael Maiello and Nicole Ridgway	"Alien Nation," *Forbes*, April 10, 2006.
Amy Leinbach Marquis	"Fenced In," *National Parks*, Spring 2008.
John F. McManus	"The Battle Against Illegal Immigration," *New American*, March 4, 2008.
Ramesh Ponnuru	"Getting Immigration Right," *National Review*, October 8, 2007.

OPPOSING
VIEWPOINTS®
SERIES

CHAPTER 4

Does Immigration Threaten National Security?

Chapter Preface

In 2004 the U.S. government inaugurated a new entry and exit program for foreign visitors. Dubbed US-VISIT, the United States Visitor and Immigrant Status Indicator Technology program was born out of concern over border and travel security after the terrorist attacks of September 11, 2001. US-VISIT, operated by the Department of Homeland Security (DHS), requires that foreigners traveling to the United States acquire passports equipped with biometric information—digital photograph and fingerprints—to accurately prove their identity. The DHS attests, "Unlike names and dates of birth, which can be changed, biometrics are unique and virtually impossible to forge." Such documents are expected to be obtained in passport-issuing bureaus in the visitor's home country and must be checked at ports of entry and exit in the United States.

Opponents of the US-VISIT system of identification complain that it makes travelers feel like criminals. In addition, foreign nations—which do not foist such procedures on American visitors—argue that the process of obtaining a US-VISIT-compliant passport is taxing and time consuming. Foreign travelers have to go through background checks and interviews in addition to the biometric data gathering in order to plan a visit to the United States. The *Washington Post* reported that the Brazilian government was so put off that it "retaliated by photographing and fingerprinting visitors from the United States." Some feel that the extensive process could deter foreign tourists from visiting the United States. American critics are also greatly aggravated by the price tag of US-VISIT. The cost to date has reached over $15 billion, and yet the DHS has stated that the operation has netted only about a thousand illegal or criminal travelers.

Defenders of the US-VISIT program state that foreign visitors are being moved through security checkpoints fairly quickly and that these travelers enjoy knowing that criminals are not stealing their identities to enter the States. Robert Mocny, a former deputy director of US-VISIT, told Congress, "We must continue to respect our visitors' privacy, treat them fairly, and enable them to pass through inspection quickly so they can enjoy their visit in our country. . . . The ability of US-VISIT to rapidly screen applicants' biometrics and biographic information through watch lists and databases means we can have security and control without impeding legitimate travelers, and we can also help protect our welcomed visitors by drastically reducing the possibility of identity theft." Mocny insisted that the advantage of US-VISIT is that instead of monitoring travelers at points of entry, the program helps create a virtual border that prescreens applicants, checks their identity at ports of entry, watches them as they move about the country, and notes their exit. Mocny warned Congress, "US-VISIT and the broader vision of a 'virtual border' cannot be left unfinished. It is the correct program at the right time, not only for the security of our country, but also for the integrity of our immigration system."

In this chapter, various critics and commentators debate whether immigration is a security threat to the United States and what government programs need to be modified to reduce the potential risk of another 9/11.

| "Terrorist organizations themselves have recognized the visa waiver program as a chink in America's defenses."

The Visa Waiver Program Is a Security Threat

Dan Stein

Dan Stein is the president of the Federation for American Immigration Reform (FAIR), a nonprofit organization that advocates immigration reform to reduce the number of legal and illegal immigrants entering the United States. Stein argues in the following viewpoint—a testimony before Congress—that the Visa Waiver Program (VWP) should be terminated. This program, which allows visitors from specific countries to travel briefly in the United States without a passport, may help terrorists gain entry to the United States, Stein contends. He maintains that forcing foreign nationals to obtain passports is a necessary—and not unduly inconvenient—step in screening out those who might wish to do harm to America and its citizens.

Dan Stein, "The Visa Waiver Program and the Screening of Potential Terrorists: Statement to the U.S. House of Representatives Committee on International Relations, Subcommittee on International Terrorism, Nonproliferation and Human Rights," *Federation for American Immigration Reform*, www.fairus.org, June 21, 2004. Reproduced by permission.

As you read, consider the following questions:

1. What fraction of the estimated 9 to 11 million illegal alien population in the United States entered the country legally, as Stein reports?

2. How does Stein refute the argument that eliminating the VWP would lead to a decrease in tourism in the United States?

3. Why does Stein believe that ending the VWP would not inconvenience American travelers overseas?

The Federation for American Immigration Reform has long been concerned that the Visa Waiver Program (VWP) endangers U.S. national security. The VWP was instituted at a time when the threat of international terrorism did not loom as ominous as it does today. It was intended to expedite travel to our country for people who were a low risk of becoming illegal aliens. Today, in the post-9/11 world, there are additional concerns that must be considered.

In this day and age, we would not consider allowing anyone—including our own citizens and VWP passport holders—to board an airplane without thoroughly screening them. It, therefore, makes no sense to let them off the plane, and into our country, without some sort of screening process. There can be little doubt that if the VWP did not exist, and all travelers except for the special provisions for Canadians and Mexicans were required to present visas, that the processes to identify and keep out potential terrorists and intending illegal aliens would be enhanced.

Terrorists in the West

Our own intelligence and law enforcement agencies acknowledge that there are large numbers of Islamic fundamentalists and persons with identified connections to al-Qaeda and other international terrorist organizations who reside in European countries that participate in the VWP. As Dr. Stephen M.

Steinlight wrote in an April 2004 publication of the Center for Immigration Studies, "Virtually every major city in Western Europe has a central mosque, funded by the Saudis, that preaches extremist Wahabbi doctrine. These mosques, that have spawned the likes of Zacharias Moussaoui and Richard Reid, are recruiting centers and financial support networks for Muslim terrorist cells." Many extremists are citizens of those countries. In addition, others connected to terrorism who reside in those countries have access to stolen or altered passports of those countries.

The terrorist organizations themselves have recognized the visa waiver program as a chink in America's defenses against their infiltration of our country. In his March 2004 book, *Bearers of Global Jihad?: Immigration and National Security After 9/11*, published by the Nixon Center, Dr. Robert S. Leiken . . . notes that, "al-Qaeda strives to recruit individuals with access to Western passports. Since September 11, jihadists have rebuilt and even extended their European operations." With large, and often radicalized, Islamic populations in many VWP countries, the failure to pre-screen citizens of any country poses a significant risk to homeland security.

The issues which must be balanced in considering whether the VWP should be abolished involve the amount of threat resulting from the existence of the program and the amount of increased security that would result from its abolishment. The ease with which terrorists may be able to enter the country at ports of entry is obviously of paramount importance, but one should not overlook the extent to which illegal residence in the United States is also facilitated by the program. The latter is relevant because the cumulative size of the illegal alien population, now estimated at 9 to 11 million persons, with about one-third of them estimated to be persons who entered legally and then stayed on illegally, provides camouflage for the operation of terrorists who are in the country.

A Useful Tool to Identify Terrorists

In assessing the national security threat represented by travelers from VWP countries it is relevant to keep in mind the following:

- the Moussaoui and Reid cases, noted above, both of whom were terrorists, traveled to the U.S. respectively on a French and United Kingdom passport,

- the emergence in European VWP countries of a breeding ground for Islamic fundamentalists, noted above,

- the role of Germany, a VWP participant, as a planning center for the September 11 terrorist attacks, and

- the fact that some of the members in the September 11 terrorist conspiracy were unable to participate in the attacks because they were denied visas.

It can be argued that, because all of the 19 September 11 terrorists received visas, the consular screening process for visa issuance is irrelevant to national security. That argument ignores both the fact that the consular screening succeeded in denying entry to some of the participants, and the fact that consular visa screening, backed up by Department of Homeland Security screening, is much more rigorous today than before September 11.

A visa interview conducted by a person who is familiar with the language, customs and documents of the visa applicant's country will always offer a greater opportunity to identify and deny a visa to a person who is not a bona fide visitor to the United States. Although there are major pressures on the visa-issuing consuls abroad, these are not as great as the pressures on the immigration and customs authorities at U.S. ports of entry. Therefore, when there is consular screening, not only is there a secondary check on the bona fides of an intending traveler and the legitimacy of the passport, it is a

Screening at the Door

I do not believe that requiring visitors who seek entry in our country to first obtain a visa is an unreasonable burden. The law permits the State Department to give aliens who appear to be credible, visas that last for 10 years. This is no greater a burden than some states impose on motorists who have to renew driver's licenses. In the high-stakes world of terrorism we now confront, it is time to eliminate the Visa Waiver Program and do what any sensible homeowner would do before opening the door to a visitor—making certain that he or she knows who they are letting in.

Michael Cutler,
"U.S. Visa Waiver Program Should End," Counterterrorism Blog,
July 10, 2005. http://counterterror.typepad.com.

check that is better informed and not as compromised by the time pressures to avoid bottlenecks at the U.S. port of entry.

Accepting the Inconvenience

Elimination of the VWP will admittedly have its costs, both monetary and the added inconvenience that will be imposed on legitimate travelers. The U.S. tourism industry argues that these costs may be harmful to their interests. As we have learned from the bitter lessons of 9/11, the price of failing to take necessary precautions is significantly higher. The loss of lives, the destruction of property and the reluctance of people to travel out of fear outweigh any additional costs and inconvenience that might rise as a result of elimination of the VWP. People have accepted the costs and inconveniences associated with modern travel, and there is every reason to believe that travelers from those countries affected will understand and accept the need to secure a visa before coming to the United States.

American businesses that depend on tourism and travel argue that national security depends on intelligence information rather than consular screening. We certainly concur. But enhanced intelligence does not negate the critical supporting role of consular screening of visa applicants in using intelligence information to screen out terrorists, in identifying falsified passports, and in applying in-country expertise to screen out persons ineligible for visas.

The concern of the travel industry that elimination of the VWP would lead to a major decrease in tourism to the U.S. and jeopardize this lucrative industry which employs many people in this country is also misplaced. The industry ignores the fact that foreign travelers to the United States do not have to obtain a U.S. visa every time they travel to the United States. Before the VWP was started, and in countries that do not now participate in the program, persons intending to travel to the United States apply for a visa at a U.S. consulate only if they did not already have one.

A One-Time Application

Visas are issued for varying periods of validity and varying numbers of entry into the United States, depending on reciprocity, country-by-country experience with visa abuse, and the judgment of the consular officer. Prior to creation of the VWP, in countries that now participate in the program, such as the United Kingdom, most citizens received visas that were indefinitely valid. In other words, a U.K. visitor to the United States would have to apply in person only once in order to be able to visit the United States over a lifetime. If we return to this system in which all visitors have to make at least one in-person application for a visa, it would have no effect on travelers who already have visas.

There would be a transitional need for persons who have never obtained a U.S. visa to apply for one, but, after that transition, only persons who are first-time visitors to the United States would have to apply. These are exactly the persons who need to be interviewed and have their travel document scrutinized by a consular officer to determine that they are bona fide visitors.

Any Foreign National Could Be a Threat

The VWP relies on an assumption that nationals of the countries that participate in the program represent a negligible threat of becoming illegal aliens in our country. Yet, there is currently no basis for that assumption. It is only in comparison to the illegal alien population from other countries that are not participants in the program, Mexico especially, that the incidence of illegal immigration from VWP countries pale by comparison.

The 1986 IRCA [Immigration Reform and Control Act] amnesty demonstrated that nationals of the VWP also become illegal residents of our country. Nearly all, if not all, of the current 27 VWP countries had nationals who applied for the amnesty. According to the Report on the Legalized Alien Population issued in March 1992, which included data on about half of the amnesty applicants, five of the VWP participating countries had more than 1,000 amnesty applicants, with the United Kingdom at the top of the list with 6,686 applicants.

It is impossible to determine the number of illegal immigrants from VWP countries since the 1986 amnesty, but immigration data reveal that in 2002 over 70 percent of the newly admitted immigrants from VWP countries were already residing in the United States. This compares with less than 64 percent of the new immigrants from non-VWP countries who similarly were already residing in the United States.

Reciprocity Concerns

There is one final argument against terminating the VWP. As noted above, visa practices are often based on reciprocity. If we were to end our program, U.S. travelers could find their ability to travel to those 27 countries without obtaining visas similarly ended. This would represent an inconvenience for U.S. travelers. However, today reciprocity plays a much smaller role in visa policies than do tourism considerations. Many countries do not require visas of U.S. visitors even though we require them of their nationals. This suggests the possibility that inconvenience to U.S. travelers as a result of a termination of the VWP could be minimal.

In summary, we find the arguments for continuing the VWP not compelling, and the national security and exclusion of intending illegal alien reasons for terminating the program persuasive. The threat to our homeland from international terrorism now and for the foreseeable future is so great that we can ill afford to perpetuate loopholes in our security system like the VWP.

> *"Extending the VWP to a small and se-*
> *lect group of countries would not com-*
> *promise the ability of the U.S. govern-*
> *ment to protect the American homeland*
> *from terrorists and others who would*
> *do us harm."*

The Visa Waiver Program Is Not a Security Threat

Daniel Griswold

The United States adopted the Visa Waiver Program (VWP) to give foreign visitors from preselected countries the right to travel to America without a passport for 90 days. Daniel Griswold states in the following viewpoint that this program needs to be expanded to give more nations access to American tourism. In Griswold's opinion, barring certain allies and otherwise friendly nations from the VWP list decreases the amount of tourist trade and sends a message that these countries are not as trusted as those nations that enjoy visa waiver status. Furthermore, Griswold argues that most of the nations asking for VWP privileges do not pose a threat to American security and should be admitted to the VWP accordingly. Daniel Griswold is the director of

the Center for Trade Policy Studies at the Cato Institute, a liber-
tarian public policy research organization.

As you read, consider the following questions:

1. What must be the refusal rate of visa applicants for a nation to currently enjoy VWP privileges, as Griswold explains?

2. Why does Griswold contend that nations such as South Korea and the Czech Republic would not be a security threat if they were granted admittance to the VWP?

3. What does Griswold say the U.S. government could do if a nation admitted to the VWP proves to be a threat to economic or national security?

D riven by legitimate but misdirected concerns about radical Islamic terrorism, current U.S. visa policy is discouraging hundreds of thousands of peaceful and well-meaning people from visiting the United States for business and pleasure—costing our country lost economic opportunities totaling millions of dollars and the goodwill of millions of people.

For most people outside the United States, the U.S. government requires that they obtain a visa before entering our country. But for residents of Canada and 27 other countries in the Visa Waiver Program [VWP], no visa is required for tourism or business visits of fewer than 90 days. The 27 countries include most countries of Western Europe, and Japan, Australia, New Zealand, Singapore, and Brunei. Another group of countries would like to join the list, but not a single country has been added since the terrorist attacks of September 11, 2001.

During a [November, 2006] stop in Tallin, Estonia, President [George W.] Bush called on Congress to extend the VWP to several more countries beyond the 27 already participating. Congress and the Bush administration should consider a prudent expansion of the list of visa waiver countries. Begun in

1986, the program has promoted tourism to the United States and expanded commercial ties with the rest of the world. Participating countries now account for two-thirds of visitors to the United States outside of Canada and Mexico.

Stimulating Tourism and Business

For a country to join the program, it must meet certain criteria. Among them, the refusal rate among current visa applicants from the country must be less than 3 percent; its citizens must be issued machine-readable passports, and its government must allow visa-free entry for U.S. citizens.

The VWP has been a boon to the U.S. economy, promoting tourism and business travel. Visitors under the program stimulate an estimated $75 billion to $100 billion in economic activity in the United States each year through travel and spending. On average, VWP visitors will spend $2,253 per visit in the United States compared with $1,274 by other visitors.

If Congress were to revoke the program for the existing 27 countries, the economic impact on the United States would be significant. According to the Commerce Department, eliminating the program would mean 3 million fewer visitors during the next five years, costing the United States $28 billion in lost economic activity during that period. Assessing the broader impact, the report concluded that revoking the program "could negatively affect U.S. relations with participating country governments, impede tourism to the United States, and increase the need for State personnel and facilities overseas." The logical implication is that extending the program to deserving countries would promote more tourism and economic activity, nurture better relations with participating countries, and free up State Department personnel and facilities overseas for more critical uses.

For tangible evidence, consider the differing experiences of Portugal and the Czech Republic. The two countries are remarkably similar in their demographics and economic relations with the United States. Their total populations and GDP per capita are almost identical. Two-way trade with the United States and the amount of U.S. foreign direct investment in each country are also quite similar (see Table . . .).

Both are members of NATO and the European Union. A key difference, however, is that Portugal gained visa waiver status before 2001, while the Czech Republic languishes outside the gate as one of the "roadmap countries." As a result, the annual number of visitors to the United States from Portugal is more than twice that of the Czech Republic.

One obvious explanation for the huge difference is the need for Czech visitors to acquire a visa. Acquiring a visa costs one hundred U.S. dollars and requires filling out numerous forms and waiting weeks and sometimes months for an interview at a consulate that may be a significant distance from a potential visitor's home. The far lower number of visitors from the Czech Republic compared with those from Portugal hints at the large number of potential visitors who are being discouraged from travel to the United States by the current moratorium on extending visa waiver status.

No Compromise of National Security

Extending the VWP to a small and select group of countries would not compromise the ability of the U.S. government to protect the American homeland from terrorists and others who would do us harm. None of the roadmap countries harbor restive populations associated even indirectly with terrorism aimed at the United States. If security concerns center on Islamic extremists, most of the roadmap countries under current consideration are home to relatively small Muslim populations.

According to the U.S. State Department's annual survey of religious freedom, South Korea, Poland, the Czech Republic, Slovakia, Hungary, and the three Baltic republics are home to a combined Muslim population of fewer than 100,000. In contrast, the number of Muslims living in the major visa waiver countries of Western Europe—Germany, France, Great Britain, the Netherlands, Italy, and Spain—is more than 13 million. If a major security worry is that Muslim extremists will be able to slip into the United States through a visa waiver country, the eight road map countries listed above are not a significant problem.

The 3-percent rejection rate threshold should not be a barrier to expanding the program. The system is designed to filter out people who would be disproportionately inclined to overstay their visas to the United States for economic reasons and thus add to the population of undocumented people here. Visa rejections on those grounds are inherently subjective, based on underinformed and largely intuitive judgments of embassy and consulate personnel.

For various reasons, South Korea and most of the Central and Eastern European countries are not likely to become major sources of illegal visa "overstayers." Those nations are generally middle- and upper-income countries. Six roadmap countries—the Czech Republic, Hungary, Poland, Slovakia, South Korea, and Greece—are members of the rich-country club, the Organization of Economic Cooperation and Development. The economic incentive for their residents to immigrate illegally to the United States is weak. For many of the European countries, their residents are already able to migrate freely to other member states of the European Union, further reducing the allure of an illegal existence in the United States.

If several thousand Koreans and Europeans did take advantage of an expanded program to overstay and settle illegally in the United States, the harm to our country would be minimal. In fact, such immigrants might actually benefit our economy by filling niches in our labor market and adding to our productive capacity. The risk of a relatively small number of visitors overstaying their visas would be far outweighed by

Visa Barriers Discourage Czech Visitors		
	Czech Republic	Portugal
Population	10.2M	10.6M
Gross Domestic Product per Capita	$20,000	$19,000
U.S. Foreign Direct Investment in Country	$2,785M	$2,712M
Two-Way Trade in Goods	$3,247M	$3,461M
Visitors to U.S.	45,671	103,473
Visa Waiver	No	Yes

TAKEN FROM: Deniel Griswold, "Expand Visa Waiver Program to Qualified Countries," *Free Trade Bulletin* No. 26, January 26, 2007.

the palpable benefits of more tourism and business visitors, enhanced foreign relations, and a redeploying of consular resources to countries where security concerns are more pressing.

Target Only Problem Nations

As a final safeguard, the U.S. government can promptly terminate a nation's participation in the program if they determine that it threatens U.S. economic or national security interests. For example, sharp economic downturns in Argentina and Uruguay beginning in 2001 raised concerns that visitors from those countries would seek to stay illegally in the United States to escape difficult conditions in their home country. As a result, Argentina was removed from the program in February 2002 and Uruguay in April 2003.

Expanding the VWP to a select list of countries would enhance national security by allowing the State Department to concentrate its resources and personnel in regions of the world where security threats are more likely to emanate. As a [2006] Congressional Research Service report summarized, "by waiving the visa requirement for high-volume/low-risk countries, consular workloads are significantly reduced, allowing for streamline operation, cost savings, and concentration of resources on greater risk nations in the visa process."

The VWP could be prudently expanded by congressional action that would allow the 3-percent rejection threshold to be temporarily waived for otherwise qualified countries. If expansion to certain countries proved an unacceptable risk to U.S. security or led to widespread violation of U.S. immigration law, any country could be promptly removed from the program à la Argentina and Uruguay. The U.S. government could also require that visitors from VWP countries submit biographical details through the Internet before departing for the United States to give the Department of Homeland Security an opportunity to compare their names to those on security watch lists. Australia has implemented such a system through its Electronic Travel Authorization process.

Tearing Down Another Cold War Barrier

Twenty years ago in Berlin, President Ronald Reagan issued his famous challenge to President [Mikhail] Gorbachev to "tear down this wall." Within three years the Berlin Wall was history. Now we have an opportunity, by extending the Visa Waiver Program to deserving countries, to complete Ronald Reagan's vision by tearing down one of the last remaining barriers of the Cold War.

In a letter to President Bush in May 2006, former Czech President and anti-communist dissident Vaclav Havel urged the United States to add his country and other proven friends of the United States to the VWP. "Contacts between Czechs and Americans are currently complicated by the asymmetrical visa requirement that subjects Czech citizens to an expensive and arduous visa application process," Havel wrote. Speaking for his country as well as others, Havel added that expanding the program would "remove what Czechs feel is an unfortunate relic of the Cold War that no longer belongs in the modern Czech-U.S. alliance. It also allows you to demonstrate to an emancipated and self-confident ally the renowned U.S. spirit of equality and fair play."

At a time when the United States is seeking not only to attract more global customers for its goods and services but also to build stronger ties to our allies, expanding the Visa Waiver Program to eligible countries offers a power tool to further both objectives.

"With all we know about the risks and costs associated with visa overstayers, it is hard to understand why [the Department of Homeland Security] has displayed so little curiosity about this population."

Aliens Who Overstay Their Visas Are a Serious Security Threat

Jessica M. Vaughan

In the following viewpoint, Jessica Vaughan argues that immigrants—both illegal and legal—who overstay their visa limits pose a danger to the United States. Vaughan states that the Department of Homeland Security has the authority and technology to track down visa overstayers, but it seems unconcerned with doing so. According to Vaughan, the government is uninterested because it favors expanding visa waivers to more foreign visitors. If visa overstayers are not rounded up, Vaughan fears that there will be more terrorists, criminals, and illegal residents pouring into the country. Jessica Vaughan is a senior policy ana-

Jessica M. Vaughan, "Weaknesses in the Visa Waiver Program: Are the Needed Safeguards in Place to Protect America?: Testimony to the U.S. Senate Judiciary Committee, Subcommittee on Terrorism, Technology and Homeland Security," *Center for Immigration Studies*, www.cis.org, February 28, 2008. Reproduced by permission.

lyst for the Center for Immigration Studies, a think tank devoted to researching the economic and social impact of immigrants in America.

As you read, consider the following questions:

1. As Vaughan writes, when did Congress first implement an entry–exit system for foreign visitors?
2. How does Vaughan use the FBI's Project Pinpoint to further her allegations against the Department of Homeland Security?
3. As Vaughan reports, about how many illegal and criminal aliens is the Immigration and Customs Enforcement agency able to remove from the U.S. population each year?

Immmigration policymakers on [Capitol] Hill and in the Executive Branch have understood for well over a decade that visa overstayers represent a significant share of the illegal alien population. Estimates range from one-third to one-half of the illegal alien population, or between four to six million illegal aliens. They present a possible national security risk—several of the 9/11 hijackers were visa overstayers, and others have been caught working in critical infrastructure facilities or other sensitive locations. They commit crimes. For example, among the most violent criminal gangsters arrested under ICE's, [Immigration and Customs Enforcement] Operation Community Shield [a 2005 initiative targeting transnational street gangs] were several murderers who entered on non-immigrant visas. In addition, like other illegal immigrants, visa overstayers are costly to taxpayers. The total net cost of illegal immigration runs about $10 billion per year, after taxes are accounted for, so the share of that cost attributable to visa overstayers is likely $3–5 billion per year.

Questionable Homeland Security Decisions

With all we know about the risks and costs associated with visa overstayers, it is hard to understand why DHS [the Department of Homeland Security], has displayed so little curiosity about this population. Most observers agree that collecting and analyzing information on visa overstayers is key to maintaining the integrity of the immigration system. Congress first mandated the development of an entry–exit system in 1996, after the first World Trade Center bombing. In addition to producing actionable enforcement leads, a true entry–exit recording system would enable policymakers to assess which travelers are not complying with the law. Visa overstay data provide information on how travelers actually behave, and are less speculative than refusal rates, which reflect the aggregate of consular officers' assessment of possible behavior. This data is important to consular officers, who crave better information to use in making visa issuance decisions. It is especially important in making an objective and sound determination of which countries might qualify for the Visa Waiver Program [VWP]. How DHS can contemplate expanding the system before the entry–exit system is ready is beyond my comprehension, but that is exactly what is happening.

As a condition for granting DHS the sole authority and discretion for determining membership in the Visa Waiver Program, last year Congress directed the agency to establish an exit recording system for air travelers that can account for at least 97% of those who depart by air. This is in addition to long-standing requirements for DHS to implement an exit recording system as part of US-VISIT [a system of issuing passports with biometric information encoded] and long-ignored requirements for DHS to produce annual estimates of how many travelers have overstayed visas and the nationality of visa overstayers (the Data Management Improvement Act of 2000 and the Visa Waiver Permanent Program Act).

The DHS Has the Capability
to Enforce Monitoring

DHS has made good progress in establishing the entry system (US-VISIT). But not only has DHS failed to move forward on establishing a true exit system, it has not made full use of those tools already in place, specifically the biographic matching system based on information collected by airlines on passenger manifests. Essentially, DHS is trying to eat its cake and hide it too—it claims that the biographic matching system fulfills the requirements of the VWP expansion law, but will not produce any reports from the system to inform the selection of countries to be included in the expansion, or to meet its obligations under the law.

The biographic matching system has been in place since the beginning of 2004. It has a number of limitations. First of all, it is maintained by the airlines, and there is no way to verify the accuracy of the information. Since it is biographic, not biometric, it cannot authenticate the identity of departing passengers. This means it would be easy for someone to create a record of leaving the country without actually leaving. Finally, DHS is not attempting to match records to determine compliance with the terms of the visa, only to any previous departures or adjustments.

It's fair for Congress to ask why, after all these years, is DHS still unable to fulfill this requirement? Since 2004, DHS has operated the Compliance Enforcement Unit (CEU), which receives and analyzes information from US-VISIT, SEVIS [Student and Exchange Visitor Information System], NSEERS [National Security entry–exit Registration System], and other sources to generate enforcement leads for ICE. CEU has provided data to the State Department for an evaluation of overstays in the H-2B guestworker program [a temporary work visa for non-immigrant foreign visitors]. It provides data to FBI agents in Philadelphia, who map the location of overstayers, along with other lawbreakers, as part of a local crime-solving effort known as Project Pinpoint. If DHS can manage to provide information of this level of detail to other agencies to use in very specific ways, why can they not produce even a basic report on the estimated number and citizenship of overstayers to help establish if certain countries are a good bet for the Visa Waiver Program?

Electronic Travel Authorization of Limited Use in Detecting Unqualified Travelers

The implementation of the Electronic Travel Authorization (ETA) process has been touted as a major security enhancement to the Visa Waiver Program. It is important to recognize that while this process will provide the opportunity for advance database checks on travelers before they arrive, and may succeed in alerting officials to the pending arrival of people who may be of interest, the ETA tool is really of very limited utility in determining the eligibility of travelers or screening out terrorists and criminals. As far as I can tell, the ETA process is simply an advance automated name check. Certainly this adds another layer and another opportunity for screening, but not much more than would be accomplished anyway at the port of entry. The port of entry screening is much more thorough because it authenticates the traveler's identity using fingerprint and digital photo matching, checks an array of security and crime databases, and includes verbal questioning.

The ETA is certainly no substitute for a consular interview. Much as a doctor can best make a diagnosis by seeing and talking with the patient, the consular interview is the best tool for evaluating the qualifications of prospective visitors. And qualifying for admission to the United States is not simply a matter of not being a known terrorist or criminal. To be admitted, visitors need to demonstrate that they have a legitimate reason for travel and that they are likely to return home. That determination simply cannot be done electronically.

Al-Qaeda Overstayers

30 to 40 percent of the total illegal population are visa overstayers. Estimates vary; and, of course, it is guesswork anyway—but educated guesswork.

So that is important to the immigration issue in general.

But specifically to the issue of terrorism, we found that a majority of the terrorists who were illegal aliens when they committed their crimes were, in fact, visa overstayers, that out of the 48 al-Qaeda operatives who committed crimes here between 1993 and 2001, 12 of them were illegal aliens when they committed their crimes, 7 of them were visa overstayers, including 2 of the conspirators in the first World Trade Center attack, one of the figures from the New York subway bomb plot, and 4 of the 9/11 terrorists. In fact, even a couple other terrorists who were not illegal when they committed their crimes had been visa overstayers earlier and had either applied for asylum or finagled a fake marriage to launder their status.

So, given the prevalence of overstays among terrorists in the United States, it is clearly an important security goal to limit this phenomenon. And there are two parts to that. One is keeping likely overstays from getting in in the first place. That is a State Department function. The second is detecting overstays once they overstay, if they get through the screen.

Mark Krikorian, testimony before House of Representatives Committee on International Relations, May 11, 2006.

Proposed Expansion Raises Security Concerns

The State Department once stated in a response to a GAO [Government Accountability Office] report, "The Department recognizes that a major reason for the [Visa Waiver] Program's success lies in the strict standards for participation." DHS's move to designate as many as nine new VWP countries this year represents a marked deviation from what has been a reasonably successful approach. The nine countries being proposed are: South Korea, the Czech Republic, Greece, Malta, Slovakia, Hungary, Lithuania, Latvia, and Estonia. While some of these countries appear to meet the criteria for the program, even under the old, stricter rules, a number of them do not. Because we currently lack the safeguards to prevent large numbers of inadmissible travelers from entering, and because we lack the ability to identify and remove those who overstay, the expansion of the program to include more than the small handful of clearly qualified countries is risky. A number of the countries on the DHS list are associated with serious law enforcement problems such as organized crime and visa fraud, and a number of the countries have large numbers of visa applicants who are not qualified and whose visitors have poor records of visa compliance.

While overstay rates in combination with other security requirements would be the best measure to determine if a country should be included in the Visa Waiver Program, in their absence DHS may continue to use refusal rates. Two of the nine proposed countries, Greece and Malta, have refusal rates below three percent, which is the old threshold for participation (along with other security factors). Another three countries have refusal rates under the new 10% threshold DHS is allowed to use: the Czech Republic (6.7%), Estonia (4%), and South Korea (4.4%). Each of these countries has its own unique problems to overcome, but on balance each presents a relatively reasonable case for consideration.

Four of the countries on the DHS list have refusal rates above the limit proscribed by the law: Lithuania (12.9%), Latvia (11.8%), Hungary (10.3%) and Slovakia (12%). Without data showing strong records of compliance, these four countries appear to be weak candidates for the VWP.

Some observers have suggested that the visa refusal rates are an unfair representation of a country's readiness for the Visa Waiver Program, and that consular officers judge applicants from these countries too harshly. Yet a new study by the Center for Immigration Studies finds the opposite—that consular officers are too lenient in issuing visas, and that issuance rates are much higher than conditions in many countries warrant, especially Eastern European countries. For one thing, the lack of feedback consular officers receive on travelers receiving visas who are later denied entry or caught overstaying causes many to underestimate the scale of the problem. In addition, many diplomats fail to appreciate the deep quality of life differences between the United States and the charming countries in which they serve—for example, a $600 a month office clerk salary may seem comfortable for Prague or Budapest, especially relative to what others there earn, but is much less attractive than what that person can earn here. Finally, the "issuance" and "customer service" culture that prevailed in the consular corps before 9/11 is still dominant today. Consular officers have little incentive to be tough or even realistic in their decisions, and face no accountability for repeatedly issuing visas to unqualified applicants. On the contrary, they are instructed to find excuses or reasons to issue, despite what the law requires.

Looking to Fast-Track VWP Applicant Nations

Pressure to help some of the VWP roadmap countries meet the refusal rate criteria could be one factor behind the recent drop in refusals in some of these countries (as happened with

Ireland in the period before its acceptance). From 2006 to 2007, the refusal rates of Lithuania and Latvia dropped by about 50% (from 27.7% to 12.9% and from 21.6% to 11.8% respectively). Over the same period Hungary's dropped from 12.7% to 10.3%, and Slovakia's went from 16% to 12%. Meanwhile, validation studies and other reports suggest overstay rates may be as high as 25–30% for citizens of some of these countries.

It has been suggested that conditions have improved in these countries sufficiently so that fewer applicants would seek to overstay in the United States, or that those who wish to move would be more likely to relocate in other European Union countries, not the United States. These claims are speculative at best. For one thing, these countries have significant diasporas in the United States to attract and shelter new illegal immigrants. Even more important, the absence of a visa requirement will almost certainly cause far more people to consider illegal immigration as an option, as there will be virtually no chance of rejection at the port of entry, as long as the traveler is not a known terrorist or criminal.

Most of the visitors from the fast-track or "road map" countries certainly are not terrorists or criminals. However, reports from U.S. and international law enforcement agencies suggest that many of them do present significant law enforcement concerns that are sure to be exacerbated if travel to the United States is made easier. For instance:

- Greece is an important gateway for illegal drugs from the Middle East and Southwest Asia;

- Organized crime is rampant throughout Eastern Europe, and several of the crime syndicates headquartered in Russia and Budapest also have operations in Philadelphia, Miami, Los Angeles, New York, Boston, and Chicago. These groups, which include the notorious Semion Mogilevich Organization and the Solntsevskaya

Organization, are involved in arms dealing, drug trafficking, uranium trafficking, murder, and visa and immigration fraud.

- Estonia, the Czech Republic, Hungary, Lithuania, and Slovakia are all home to significant illegal drug production operations;

- The Czech Republic, Estonia, Greece and Hungary all provide bases for major drug trafficking organizations;

- A number of Lithuanians have been convicted recently in the United States in major immigration fraud-related conspiracies.

- Korean criminal enterprises are known for trafficking crystal methamphetamine and heroin, extortion, gambling, alien smuggling, prostitution, and money laundering, and have established particularly strong footholds in Hawaii and the west coast.

In at least one Eastern European country, an organized crime syndicate has successfully hijacked the U.S. diversity visa, or visa lottery, application process. The syndicate used stolen data from a university student database to populate electronic visa lottery applications. Then it intercepted the winners' letters from a local post office, and coerced the unsuspecting winners into completing the green card applications, sometimes with new spouses provided by the syndicate. Upon arrival in the United States, the winners reportedly remained under the hold of the syndicate and were forced into ongoing criminal activity.

Holes in the System

Although VWP countries are required to develop more secure passports and share data on lost and stolen passports, serious questions remain about the integrity of passports throughout the European Union, and especially in the "new" European countries. In 2006, a BBC reporter was able to obtain and use 20 different EU [European Union] passports, (including Czech, Estonian and Latvian passports) paying between 250–1,500 pounds Sterling apiece. Her Estonian passport was registered on the Interpol database of stolen passports, but was not detected as stolen at a port of entry. It probably goes without saying that if a BBC reporter can travel at will on stolen or altered European passports, so can a terrorist.

The United States has long had a problem with prostitution sustained through human trafficking. It is worth noting that, according to government officials, some of the prostitution services trade is accomplished relatively openly, with prostitutes from Korea coming and going from the United States legally on regular B visas, rather than being trafficked in the traditional sense. Obviously Korea's membership in the VWP will facilitate this phenomenon.

All of these examples suggest that opening up admissions to the United States from this group of countries within a short time frame, without adequate safeguards in place, is inviting an increase in illegal immigration and organized criminal activity.

Interior Enforcement Lacking

Besides lacking adequate screening to prevent the entry of terrorists, criminals and illegal immigrants, the United States devotes relatively few resources to identifying and removing illegal immigrants, or to keeping them from becoming established here. While many visitors lie through their teeth to the consular officer and port of entry inspector about their plans, others do not decide to stay until after they arrive and realize how easy it is to work and live as if they were here legally.

The immigration enforcement agency (ICE) has just a few thousand special agents and deportation officers to cope with an illegal alien population of 12 million plus tens of thousands of criminal aliens who are not here illegally but are removable because they have committed serious crimes. Currently, the agency is capable of removing only about 200,000–250,000 illegal and criminal aliens per year. Only a handful of states require employers to verify the immigration status of new workers, and workplace enforcement is not the top priority for ICE, so few employers feel any urgency to comply voluntarily with the laws forbidding the hiring of illegal workers. A number of states still issue drivers licenses to illegal aliens and temporary visitors. These documents can be used to obtain employment, bank accounts, and firearms, among other trappings of a legal existence. Even if DHS is able to determine which visitors overstay, there is little chance that ICE will act on the information.

So while the expansion of the Visa Waiver Program may serve foreign policy goals and benefit certain foreign travelers, the expansion comes at a price. This price will be paid by those Americans who become victims of crimes committed by people taking advantage of the lack of visa controls, by those who lose job opportunities to new illegal immigrants overstaying their welcome, and by taxpayers who must shoulder the burden of public services, criminal justice expenses, and increased immigration law enforcement that will be necessary as a result. Congress must do what it can to try to reduce the security and fiscal cost of the program by insisting that DHS fulfill its obligations to implement a genuine exit recording system [and] produce the best possible overstay estimates, along with the other security requirements in the authorizing legislation. In addition, while there is no statutory requirement for this, the pending expansion of the VWP should be accompanied by an infusion of additional resources for law enforcement as well as the implementation of measures, such as mandatory verification of immigration status in the workplace, that will discourage visa overstayers, and all prospective illegal immigrants, from settling here.

"We must recognize that any effort to find and deport overstays will have little to do with fighting terrorism."

Aliens Who Overstay Their Visas Are Not a Serious Security Threat

Margaret D. Stock

In the following viewpoint, Margaret D. Stock, a professor of law at the United States Military Academy, informs a House of Representatives subcommittee that immigration and border controls need to be improved to keep terrorists from entering the United States. She maintains that focusing on this line of defense is more important than trying to track down immigrants who overstay their visas. According to Stock, most visa overstayers are simply seeking work and are not interested in terrorism. While Stock agrees that the Department of Homeland Security could enhance measures to deport visa overstayers, she believes that it would be wiser to devote more resources to turning terrorists away at consulates and at the border.

Margaret D. Stock, "Visa Overstayers: Can We Bar the Terrorist Door?" *Statement to the U.S. House Committee on International Relations, Subcommittee on Oversight and Investigations*, May 11, 2006. Reproduced by permission of the author.

As you read, consider the following questions:

1. How does Stock characterize the majority of visa overstayers in the United States?

2. Why does Stock believe the REAL ID Act will degrade
efforts to locate visa overstayers?

3. How does Stock wish to improve immigration laws to
help those immigrants already in the United States gain
lawful citizenship?

I am honored to be appearing before you [members of a
House of Representatives subcommittee] this afternoon to
discuss the issue of "Visa Overstayers: Can We Bar the Terrorist Door?" This hearing could not be more important or timely
because it comes as our nation is engaged in an important debate about how we should reform our immigration laws. This
hearing can help us focus on the central issues that our nation
must address successfully if we are to enhance our security
and thrive as a nation. Hopefully, we can clarify the major issues at stake, judge where we have succeeded and failed, and
question any false assumptions we may hold. For example, we
must be willing to take a hard look at the measures we have
taken to enhance our security and evaluate honestly whether
or not they actually make us safer, and whether they are worth
the cost. In addition, we must acknowledge that we cannot
enhance our security unilaterally, and must work with other
nations—this is an area where this Committee can make important contributions. Most of all, we must realize that in
these times of unprecedented challenges, we must work together.

You asked me to address the threat that visa irregularities
and overstays pose to the United States, especially in light of
the War on Terror; the weaknesses of the overstay tracking
system; the risks to domestic security; and what might be
done to resolve the overstay problem. I want to make three
key points.

Using Effective Tools

First, we secure our borders best by enhancing our intelligence capacity. We certainly need effective monitoring of status compliance within the United States combined with effective exit controls when it makes sense from a cost-benefit perspective; I support the Department of Homeland Security's efforts in this regard. Yet visa overstayers are a very tiny piece of the security picture; very few visa overstayers are terrorists, and focusing too many resources on visa overstayers means that we neglect more effective measures, such as improving our intelligence capacity. Going after all visa overstayers is not a cost-effective way to stop terrorists; in fact, such an effort would likely divert resources better used on more focused efforts, such as the use of immigration information to enhance our intelligence on terrorists and their networks. In addition, US VISIT [a system of issuing passport with biometric information encoded], the system that is supposed to let us track overstays, has been plagued with problems and delays, and the REAL ID Act [which imposed authentication technology on driver's licenses and state ID cards] has handicapped our ability to identify and find people within our borders. National security is most effectively enhanced by improving the mechanisms for identifying actual terrorists, not by implementing harsher immigration laws or blindly treating all foreigners as potential terrorists. Comprehensively reforming our immigration laws will help us to identify those who are here, and reduce significantly the number of visa overstayers.

Moving the Defenses

Second, we need to make our borders our last line of defense. If we are chasing after visa overstayers in order to stop terrorists, we have already in essence lost the fight. This approach assumes that we have already allowed the terrorists into the country. Once terrorists are inside the United States, it is very hard to find them, particularly now that we have decided to restrict the issuance of drivers' licenses and state identification documents severely. In the past, we could locate foreigners within our borders by using the drivers' license databases; that tool has now been degraded. Thus, we are forced to look to our physical borders as the next best option. And yet the physical borders of the United States should be our last line of defense because terrorism does not spring up at our borders. Rather than trying to chase visa overstayers, we should be focusing our efforts on getting resources to the consulates; providing the consulates with adequate, trained staff; and giving consulates access to accurate databases when they make the crucial decision to give someone a visa in the first place.

Immigration Reform to Correct Errors

Third, comprehensive immigration reform is an essential component of enhanced security. Our current immigration system is an obstacle to enhancing our security because it is dysfunctional. Visa overstayers are a function of the dysfunctional system that we have right now. The vast majority of people who overstay their visas are not terrorists; many are awaiting approval of an adjustment application; hoping that an immigrant visa number will become current; are afraid to leave the United States for fear of triggering a 3-year, 10-year, or permanent bar; or have become "overstays" through some bureaucratic glitch or a failure of their sponsor to file the correct paperwork. Allocating massive resources to find and deport these people makes little sense in a time when we have a far greater problem with poor intelligence on terrorists, an inability to disseminate that intelligence to the agents who need it, and a lack of consular resources to screen visa applicants properly. Once people are in the country, however, it is far easier and more cost-effective to tackle the visa overstay problem with a program to get overstays to come forward voluntarily through comprehensive immigration reform than to try to find them without their cooperation.

Finding the Right Focus for Border Security

In this mission to secure our borders, we need to grapple with the following questions:

1. What security measures are most effective—and cost-effective—in preventing attacks? If we are to succeed in reducing our vulnerability to further terrorist attacks, we must focus our attention and resources on the gaps in intelligence gathering and information sharing that allowed nineteen terrorists to enter the United States. National security is most effectively enhanced by improving the mechanisms for identifying actual terrorists, not by implementing harsher immigration laws or blindly treating all foreigners as potential terrorists. Policies and practices that fail to properly distinguish between terrorists and others take us down the wrong path as ineffective security tools that do more harm than good. Comprehensively reforming our immigration laws is an essential tool to

help us distinguish between those who mean to do us harm and those who are here to fill our labor market needs and re-unite with close family members.

2. What is the role of our "borders" in enhancing security? When people refer to our "borders," they usually mean the geographic boundaries that separate the United States from Canada and Mexico. Yet to enhance our security we must make our physical borders the last line of defense against ter-rorism, not the first. We must pursue initiatives including multilateral strategies with Canada and Mexico to create a North American Perimeter Safety Zone, and increase the use of pre-clearance and pre-inspection programs that provide U.S. officials the opportunity to check passengers for admis-sion before those passengers board a flight to the United States (while including safeguards to allow asylum protection for those who truly deserve it). We must also provide more re-sources to our overseas consulates, giving those who make ini-tial visa decisions the tools they need to make the right deci-sions.

Our government has been touting the United States Visitor and Immigrant Status Indicator Technology program (US VISIT) as a tool that will help to make us safer by identi-fying terrorists. While US VISIT can help to identify people, its utility as a security tool is unclear. On the issue of over-stays, US VISIT is not much help. Once someone is in the United States and fails to depart timely, US VISIT does nothing to help us find them. The only method of finding such overstays is (1) by accident, or (2) by checking other, internal databases that might tell us the location of the over-stays. We have crippled our capacity to find such people by enacting REAL ID, because once REAL ID goes into effect, we will no longer be able to find overstays through state driver's license databases. While other databases such as ChoicePoint can provide some alternative information that might allow us to find people, these databases are not nearly as reliable as the state DMV [Department of Motor Vehicles] records were prior to enactment of REAL ID. . . .

Reforming Laws to Aid Immigration

3. What is the role of immigration in the post–September 11 world? Because all nineteen of the September 11th terrorists were foreigners, some observers have been quick to blame our vulnerability to terrorist attacks on lax immigration laws. While such a response was predictable, it was misguided and has inevitably resulted in overreaction. Although the attacks of September 11th revealed serious management and resource deficiencies in the bureaucracies that administer our borders, U.S. immigration laws in and of themselves did not increase our vulnerability to attack. In fact, U.S. immigration laws already are among the toughest in the world and have long provided the federal government with broad powers to prevent anti-American terrorists from entering or residing in the United States. A careful analysis of the September 11th attacks reveals that deficiencies in U.S. intelligence collection and information sharing, not immigration laws, prevented the terrorists' plans from being discovered. . . .

President [George W.] Bush has been eloquent in his recognition that immigration is in America's self-interest, and that "one of the primary reasons America became a great power in the 20th century is because we welcomed the talent and the character and the patriotism of immigrant families." The President correctly recognizes that our current immigration system makes more difficult the urgent task of securing the homeland. Importantly, President Bush also succinctly identifies a problem that needs immediate attention when he said that "[a]s a nation that values immigration and depends on immigration, we should have immigration laws that work and make us proud. Yet today we do not." Our immigration laws do not make us proud.

4. Is an "enforcement only" approach sufficient in itself to secure our borders and enhance our security? No. Our current immigration laws do not make sense, do not make us safer, do not support our economy, and do not reflect our tradition as a nation of immigrants. It is my view that to secure our borders and effectively reform our immigration laws we need comprehensive immigration reform that includes, along with a worker program, an earned adjustment and family backlog reduction. People who work hard, pay taxes, and contribute to the U.S. should be allowed to obtain permanent residence and pursue a path to citizenship. Reform should stabilize the workforce of U.S. employers, encourage people to come out of the shadows to be scrutinized by our government, and allow immigrants to work and travel legally and be treated equally. Many have been here for years, are paying taxes, raising families (typically including U.S. citizen and lawful permanent resident spouses and children), contributing to their communities and are essential to the industries within which they work. In order to unite families and keep them together, appropriate waivers must be available for grounds of admissibility and deportability. In addition, our immigration system has been characterized by long backlogs in family-based immigration and long delays in business-based immigration. Illegal immigration is a symptom of a system that fails to reunify families and address economic conditions in the U.S. and abroad. To ensure an orderly future process, our system must reduce bureaucratic obstacles and undue restrictions to permanent legal immigration. Developing an increased legal migration flow will make immigration more orderly and legal. It also will allow more people to reunite with their families and work legally in the U.S., and would facilitate fair, equitable, and efficient immigration law, policy, and processing. It is essential to make legal future immigration that otherwise will happen illegally. . . .

Little to Do with Fighting Terrorism

5. How do we resolve the overstay problem? We resolve the overstay problem through better interior enforcement—to find and track those who overstay their visas, we must have accurate data on who enters the United States and if they depart. If they do not depart, we must try to obtain the most accurate data necessary to find them. Unfortunately, DHS [the Department of Homeland Security] does not have accurate data—within its own systems—to determine who is an overstay and where the overstays are. When and if the US VISIT exit feature is ever fully implemented, DHS should have data on those who have not departed in a timely fashion—but DHS must still rely on other sources of information to find any overstays. To this end, it was a mistake to enact REAL ID, which will deprive us of valuable interior enforcement data. . . . Yet in the end, we must recognize that any effort to find and deport overstays will have little to do with fighting terrorism.

│ *"The border is wide open, and anyone*
│ *who wants to can easily enter the*
│ *United States covertly."*

Illegal Immigrants Are a Threat to National Security

Jan C. Ting

Jan C. Ting is a professor of law at Temple University in Phila-
delphia. He argues in the following viewpoint that criminals and
terrorists can easily enter the United States through the nation's
porous borders. Although Ting agrees that most illegal aliens are
not terrorists, the number of immigrants crossing the borders
provides excellent cover for the few that are. Ting believes the
United States could do better in border security and deportation,
but he maintains that politicians typically lack the will to enact
stricter immigration laws.

As you read, consider the following questions:

1. According to Ting, of those illegal immigrants captured
   in 2004–2005, to what "special interest" country did the
   most OTM (other than Mexican) immigrants belong?

Jan C. Ting, "Immigration and National Security," *Orbis*, vol. 50, Winter 2005, pp. 41–
43, 45–52. Copyright © 2005 Elsevier B.V. All rights reserved. Reproduced with permission from Elsevier, conveyed through Copyright Clearance Center, Inc.

2. As Ting states, politicians typically are hesitant to tighten border security and immigration laws because they receive pressure from what two sources?

3. What are some of the ways the author suggests the United States take action to secure the border and round up illegal aliens?

The July 7, 2005, terror bombings in London and additional terrorist attempts there since then have brought new attention to the Islamist threat. They also highlighted the striking difference between U.S. and European concerns over the Islamist threat. In Europe, the greatest concern is the threat from its own resident immigrant population—particularly the young second and third generations, born in Europe. In the United States, the greatest concern is not its own population, but the threat of those sent from abroad to attack America.

Europe is now paying the price for open borders, past and present non-enforcement of immigration laws, and overly generous asylum policies. Despite government efforts to integrate Muslims, Europe's high-tax, high-unemployment, and high-welfare-benefits economic model has led to alienation among Europe's growing Muslim minority and a lack of economic and cultural integration. With acts of violence from Muslim citizens in Europe increasing in number and scale, many Europeans feel that the Islamist threat needs to be addressed at home, not in Iraq.

But four years after 9/11, America's national borders remain open and uncontrolled. Our government seems unconcerned about this, even as it spends billions of dollars and thousands of lives in Iraq and Afghanistan fighting terrorism, and even as it worries about protecting the nation's ports, power supply, mass transit, and every other possible target against terrorist threats. The border with Mexico poses particular problems, but so too do our visa-waiver program and our rules governing dual citizenship.

Flood of Illegal Immigration

The Pew Hispanic Center reported in September 2005 that illegal immigrants now outnumber legal immigrants to the United States. Every night, thousands of foreigners covertly enter the United States, and we have little idea who they are. Those we do intercept provide us with an idea of how many are illegally crossing the borders to enter the United States. The official estimate is that the U.S. Border Patrol apprehends 1 out of every 4 illegal border crossers. But current and former Border Patrol officers say that the ratio of those intercepted is much lower—probably more like 1:8 or 1:10. The number getting in is always many times higher than the number of those who are apprehended. And because of the immigrants' remittances of U.S. dollars back to their home country, Mexico in particular has been supportive of its citizens who choose to enter the U.S. illegally.

Table 1 shows Border Patrol apprehensions for fiscal years (ending September 30) 2000–05. The total number of apprehensions was highest in 2000 and then declined over the next three years, following 9/11. It then rose again in 2004 and 2005, after President [George W.] Bush announced his proposal for guest-worker amnesty in January 2004. Apprehensions along the southern border make up about 97–98 percent of total apprehensions. Most of those apprehended near the United States' southern border are Mexicans, but there are also numerous "Other than Mexicans," or OTMs.

As Mexicans have known for years, the border is wide open, and anyone who wants to can easily enter the United States covertly. According to research by Wayne Cornelius of the Center for Comparative Immigration Studies at the University of California–San Diego, 92 percent of Mexicans seeking to enter the United States illegally eventually succeed. . . .

Potentially Dangerous Illegals

The overwhelming majority of the millions of illegals ... are not terrorists. But the sea of incoming illegal aliens provides a cover and a culture in which terrorists can hide, and a reliable means of entry. We need only recall that the Madrid train bombers [who struck in 2004] resided easily in Spain (some came from Morocco, where Spanish is widely spoken) to appreciate that many Islamist terrorists are fluent in Spanish. Border Patrol apprehension figures show that among the OTMs apprehended in 2004 and 2005 were hundreds of persons from 35 "special interest" countries, almost all of which are Muslim. They include Afghanistan, Egypt, Iran, Iraq, Lebanon, Saudi Arabia, Somalia, Sudan, Syria, and Yemen; the number-one country in the group, with the largest number of aliens apprehended, is Pakistan. Again, these are just the apprehensions: for every alien apprehended entering the United States illegally, an estimated 3 to 9 others succeed.

Another threat to national security is presented by the significant number of violent criminals who are able to enter the U.S. illegally. In Los Angeles, two-thirds of all outstanding fugitive felony warrants, and 95 percent of outstanding fugitive homicide warrants, are for illegal aliens. The Mexican government refuses to extradite its criminals to the United States, where they would face the death penalty, because the Mexican constitution does not permit capital punishment. In October 2001, the Mexican Supreme Court ruled that life imprisonment also violates the Mexican constitution. So illegal aliens committing serious crimes in the United States, including the murder of police officers (for example, Los Angeles County deputy sheriff David March, who was shot to death in 2002 during a routine traffic stop) can and do seek refuge in Mexico, from which extradition is impossible unless U.S. prosecutors agree to seek only a determinate sentence. California prosecutors estimate that as many as 360 individuals who have committed murder or other serious crimes in the state

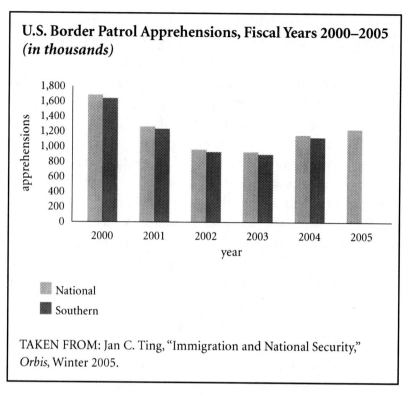

U.S. Border Patrol Apprehensions, Fiscal Years 2000–2005 (in thousands)

Legend:
- National
- Southern

TAKEN FROM: Jan C. Ting, "Immigration and National Security," *Orbis*, Winter 2005.

have not been extradited. An estimated 60 fugitives charged with or wanted for murder in Los Angeles County are believed to be at large in Mexico.

Nothing Done to Stem the Tide

The main barrier to tightening the border is the absence of political will to take any effective action to stem the tide of illegal immigration. On no other issue is the gap wider between the views of ordinary Americans, who overwhelmingly want to see the uncontrolled influx of illegal aliens halted, and those of the national political elite of both parties, who overwhelmingly feel that nothing can or should be done about our porous borders.

Politicians are pressured on two fronts when it comes to addressing the illegal alien population. First, American business, which is an important source of campaign funds, counts on plentiful, cheap labor. Illegal immigration serves its need, and also helps keep the wages of competing American and legal resident workers in check. And illegal immigrants offer revenue opportunities to many other businesses. Some U.S. banks are even granting mortgages to illegal immigrants. The other major influence on politicians is electoral: the fear that any action to restrict illegal immigration will create a backlash among the growing number of ethnic voters. However, this fear may be misplaced. It is precisely those who have recently immigrated legally to the United States who feel most keenly the competition from illegal alien labor and the impact of that competition on their own wages. But the two considerations, business and political, act together to maintain a political majority in favor of doing nothing to effectively curb illegal immigration. . . .

While it will be difficult to secure our entire 2,000-mile long southern border, there is plenty that we could do if only we had the political will to do so. We can put more people on the border, either using volunteers like the Minutemen, or using the U.S. Army Reserve and the border states' National Guards. We can resume worksite raids to arrest illegal aliens. And we can make employer sanctions work. A few years ago a pilot project was carried out to see whether employers would comply with a requirement to verify that a prospective employee's social security or other work authorization number presented by the alien was in fact a legally issued number. The project had good results but was never made mandatory. Today it might be done through the Internet, to be even faster and less burdensome for employers.

But the most effective thing that could be done is to change the cost/benefit calculation of aliens considering illegal entry to the United States. The poor are as capable as anyone of determining what is in their best interests. If we allow the situation to continue where the benefits of illegal entry into the U.S. are large, with plentiful job opportunities available to illegal aliens, while the risks of apprehension and deportation are low, potential border-crossers will make the same decision that anyone would make in their position. We cannot blame them for coming to the United States illegally in all the circumstances: they are making rational decisions which we might also make if we were in their shoes. The blame for illegal immigration properly belongs on U.S. political leaders, who enable and protect the flow of illegal aliens into the United States. . . .

The Visa-Waiver Program

Prior to 1986, the United States required visas of nearly all foreigners traveling to the United States, the exceptions being Canadians and Mexicans with border-crossing cards. To obtain a U.S. visa, a foreigner was required to apply for one at a U.S. consulate abroad, submitting his or her foreign passport, which allowed inspection of the passport to determine whether it was counterfeit or stolen, and an opportunity to ask questions before issuing a visa, or withholding a visa in appropriate cases. To board an airplane headed to the United States, a foreign national had to show a U.S. visa in his or her passport.

But in 1986, the U.S. Congress enacted a reciprocal visa-waiver program to allow the citizens of certain favored countries, mostly in Europe and now numbering 27, to enter the U.S. for up to 90 days without a visa, and vice versa. (In order for a country to be eligible for the program, the refusal rate for nonimmigrant visas for its citizens cannot exceed 3 percent.) Visa-waiver entrants may board an airplane to the United States merely by showing their passport. Visa waiver had long been sought by the U.S. tourism industry and by the airlines, and was also supported by the U.S. State Department, the staff of which was freed from having to process visa applications. (Visa-waiver entrants have lately numbered around 13 million per year.)

Who else was able to enter the United States without a U.S. visa using visa waiver? Zacarias Moussaoui, sometimes referred to as the 20th hijacker, entered the U.S. before 9/11 by showing his French passport. Moussaoui, who was arrested while taking lessons in Minnesota on flying a commercial airplane, admits to being an Al Qaeda agent. Richard Reid, the "shoe bomber," was able to board an airplane headed for the United States without a U.S. visa by showing his British passport. And one of the 1993 World Trade Center bombers, Ramsi Yusuf, was able to enter the U.S. through visa waiver after presenting a counterfeit European passport.

One might think that after 9/11, the visa-waiver program would have been eliminated. But its supporters swung into action to defend the program. At House Judiciary Committee hearings held in February 2002, witnesses testified that 9/11 changed nothing and that the case for visa waiver was as sound as ever. The number of entrants intent on mass murder who had entered the United States under visa waiver was declared to be statistically insignificant, and persons deemed unacceptable upon inspection on arrival could always be turned away. But how would this latter mechanism help against someone such as Reid, who boarded with the intent of blowing up the airplane?

Congress tried to demonstrate concern by requiring better passports of visa-waiver applicants. The USA Patriot Act required that by October 2003, visa-waiver applicants present machine-readable passports, but implementation was delayed until June 26, 2005. Deadlines for additional requirements under the Enhanced Border Security and Visa Reform Act of 2002 have been extended to October 26, 2005, for inclusion of a digital photo, and to October 26, 2006, for new passports issued by visa-waiver countries to be e-passports equipped with integrated computer chips capable of storing other biometric information. It is not clear, however, how these passport requirements mitigate the national security threat presented by visa waiver.

Especially since the London bombings and with our growing awareness of the large Islamic populations in Europe qualifying for visa waiver, commentators have begun to note the danger visa-waiver presents, since it permits entrants from nations known to have populations of Islamist terrorists, such as Spain, Germany, France, and the UK. But observers often conclude that nothing can be done because ending visa waiver and reverting to pre-1986 visa requirements would adversely impact the airline and tourist industries and burden our State Department with visa applications. Washington's consensus on visa waiver is the same as it is on our porous border: nothing can be done.

Indefinite Permanent Residence and Dual Citizenship

When a legal immigrant is admitted to the United States, he or she becomes a legal permanent resident (LPR) and receives what is commonly referred to as a green card. Typically, after five years of residence, LPRs become eligible for U.S. citizenship, and it has always been U.S. policy to encourage them to apply for citizenship and to naturalize. Doing so is not required, however, and perhaps it should be. The current policy allows millions of non-citizens who owe no loyalty to the United States to reside and work here permanently. A limitation on the duration of LPR status, perhaps to five years or as long as a citizenship application is pending, would encourage and facilitate the assimilation of immigrants.

Current U.S. policy actually encourages dual citizenship and the divided loyalty that comes with it. Unless U.S. citizens explicitly give up their citizenship, they may vote in foreign elections, serve in a foreign army hostile to the United States, or take an oath of allegiance to a foreign power—even if that oath includes a renunciation of all other loyalty—without relinquishing their U.S citizenship. Under current law, many benefits flow from dual nationality. These include the ability to carry and travel on two different passports, to work freely in each country without specific authorization, and to transmit dual citizenship to one's children. Although the Supreme Court has ruled that U.S. citizenship may not be involuntarily removed if a citizen intends to retain it, Congress could legislate and State Department give appropriate notifications that certain specified actions inherently express a citizen's intent to relinquish U.S. citizenship.

End the Inaction

The illegal immigrant himself or herself is not primarily to blame for the tide of illegal immigration which conceals and facilitates the presence of those hostile to our national security and interests. The problem continues to be the lack of political will among our leaders in Washington to recognize and respond to the flaws in our immigration system. Concerned citizens who have already written multiple letters to their elected representatives should consider running for elected office themselves on an anti-illegal immigration platform. They don't have to win, but only use the occasion to get politicians to see that their inaction on immigration reform could affect the results on election day.

Periodical Bibliography

The following articles have been selected to supplement the diverse views presented in this chapter.

The Hill	"Border-Security Plan Carries Steep Costs," June 14, 2006. http://thehill.com.
Jim Kouri	"Visa Overstays," *American Chronicle*, June 13, 2005. www.americanchronicle.com.
Roberto Lovato	"Immigrants Regroup," *Nation*, November 13, 2006.
Alexandra Marks	"A Harder Look at Visa Overstayers," *Christian Science Monitor*, February 5, 2002.
Barry Newman	"How Tools of War on Terror Ensnare Wanted Citizens," *Wall Street Journal*, October 31, 2005.
George Packer	"Keep Out," *New Yorker*, October 16, 2006.
Natsu Taylor Saito	"The Costs of Homeland Security," *Radical History Review*, Fall 2005.
Mary Beth Sheridan	"Immigration Law as Anti-Terrorism Tool," *Washington Post*, June 13, 2005.
Wall Street Journal	"Coming to America," August 2, 2007.
Roger Yu	"U.S. Loosens Rules for Foreign Visitors as Travel Dries Up," *USA Today*, November 17, 2008.

For Further Discussion

Chapter 1

1. Becky Akers and Donald J. Boudreaux argue that an increase in the number of workers, as a result of immigration to America, will increase the efficiency of production, which will in turn create higher wages and improve the economy in the long run. Art Thompson provides many examples of ways in which he believes illegal immigrants hurt the economy. Review these articles and decide whether you believe immigration helps or hurts the economy. Use examples from the viewpoints to support your answer.

2. To support the argument that immigration has negatively affected the African American community, Frank Morris provides examples of that impact. Rakesh Kochhar instead provides statistics to prove his argument that immigration alone cannot be singled out as having a negative impact on any group of workers. Which style of argument do you find more convincing? Do you respond more to Morris's more emotionally based argument or to Kochhar's statistics? Explain your answer using specific quotes from the viewpoints.

3. Much of the debate over immigrant use of social services revolves around a question of how much these individuals pay in taxes to support those services. Steven A. Camarota argues that immigrants do not pay enough in taxes proportionate to the amount of services they draw. Shikha Dalmia argues that often immigrants pay much more in taxes than they will ever be able to claim in services because, in the case of illegal immigrants, they do not have the proper documentation to utilize certain services.

Whose argument do you find more convincing? Does either author leave out important points that the other addresses? Should individuals' use of social services be based on the amount of taxes they pay or the need they have for those services? Support your view with quotes from the viewpoints.

Chapter 2

1. Many Americans—including former President George W. Bush—believe that immigrants should be compelled to learn English as part of their citizenship requirements. Kenneth Blackwell argues that English is necessary to actively participate in the public sphere, but Lloyd Garver maintains that such praiseworthy claims actually mask a fear of foreigners. Do you think Garver is correct in his assertion? Explain why or why not.

2. What evidence does Christine Rossell use to support her argument that English immersion classes benefit immigrant students? What evidence do Margaret Adams and Kellie M. Jones cite to make the opposite claim? Whose argument do you find more convincing? Be specific in explaining what claims or statistics were most persuasive and be sure to address Adams and Jones's suggestion that most English immersion teachers are not trained or prepared to teach SEI curricula.

Chapter 3

1. The building of a border fence was a topical issue throughout the presidency of George W. Bush. After reading the viewpoints by Duncan Hunter and Melanie Mason, decide whether you think a longer, stronger border fence will deter illegal immigration across the southern U.S. border. Be sure to frame your answer both in terms of economic and human rights concerns.

2. Because immigrants come to the United States in search of jobs, Robert Rector maintains that an electronic employment verification system is the most accurate and significant tool the government and businesses can use to deter illegal immigration. How does Tom DeWeese counter that assertion? What fears does DeWeese have that extend beyond the immigration debate? Explain whether you believe DeWeese's fears are justified.

3. Harry Binswanger advocates that America should adopt immigration policies that would effectively open all borders to however many immigrants wish to live and work in the country. In this common libertarian view, Binswanger claims that the larger influx of immigrants will allow the nation to become even more prosperous because there will be a larger labor pool to drive business and industry. Vin Suprynowicz, who also professes a libertarian agenda, asserts that this idealism does not match reality. He states that uncontrolled immigration has already led to overcrowding, poverty, and an ongoing contest for the limited number of jobs available in the United States. Whose opinion do you find more credible? Explain, using examples from the viewpoints.

Chapter 4

1. The Visa Waiver program was designed by the government to allow foreign nationals from "friendly" nations to travel in the United States without a passport. The program was partly conceived as a goodwill gesture that America extended to allied nations to show that people from these countries were not considered a threat to U.S. security. Dan Stein argues that, in the age of terrorism, the Visa Waiver program is outmoded and dangerous because America cannot be sure that all people from "friendly" nations are indeed "friendly." He claims terrorist organizations have already exploited the Visa Waiver pro-

gram as a means of easy access to the United States. Do you agree with Stein's cautionary argument? Or do you concur with Daniel Griswold who believes the Visa waiver program is necessary to keep up good relations with America's allies? Explain your answer.

2. Margaret D. Stock asserts that the U.S. government should invest more effort in keeping dangerous aliens away at the borders than to track down potentially dangerous aliens who have overstayed their visas. In Stock's view, most visa overstayers are simply looking to work and live in the United States and are not engaging in terrorist activities. Do you think Stock's viewpoint lacks appropriate cautiousness in a post 9/11 world? Explain your answer drawing examples from Stock's viewpoint as well as that of Jessica Vaughan.

3. Jan C. Ting states that America could do more to curb illegal immigration if politicians had the will to pass necessary legislation. Do you believe that less is being done to stem illegal immigration because politicians are giving in to the pro-illegal immigration coalition that Ting describes? Explain what reasons might lie behind America's apparent unwillingness to take a stronger hand in addressing illegal immigration.

Organizations to Contact

The editors have compiled the following list of organizations concerned with the issues debated in this book. The descriptions are derived from materials provided by the organizations. All have publications or information available for interested readers. The list was compiled on the date of publication of the present volume; the information provided here may change. Be aware that many organizations take several weeks or longer to respond to inquiries, so allow as much time as possible.

American Civil Liberties Union (ACLU)
125 Broad Street, 18th Floor, New York, NY   10004
(212) 607-3300 • fax: (212) 607-3318
Web site: www.aclu.org

The ACLU is an organization dedicated to preserving and upholding the civil rights guaranteed to all people in the United States by the U.S. Constitution and Bill of Rights. With regional offices nationwide, the ACLU seeks to provide all individuals equal services regardless of race, sex, religion, or national origin. The ACLU Immigrants' Rights Project was founded in 1987 specifically to address issues such as detention and deportation, due process, search and seizure, and workplace rights. Information on current projects by the ACLU as well as immigration-related fact sheets, publications, and Supreme Court decisions can be read online.

American Friends Service Committee (AFSC)
1501 Cherry Street, Philadelphia, PA   19102
(215) 241-7000 • fax: (215) 241-7275
e-mail: afscinfo@afsc.org
Web site: www.afsc.org

AFSC is a service organization that seeks to promote development, social justice, and peace worldwide. While the beliefs of the organization are rooted in the Quaker faith, the organization reaches out to individuals of all backgrounds and faiths. AFSC believes that current immigration policies in the United States are inhumane and unfair to individuals who immigrate to the country, even if they lack proper documentation. The AFSC provides publications of its calls for policy reform as well as in-depth reports exploring the issues of legal and illegal immigration.

American Immigration Control Foundation (AIC Foundation)

222 West Main Street, PO Box 525, Monterey, VA   24465
(540) 468-2022 • fax: (540) 468-2024
e-mail: aicfndn@htcnet.org
Web site: www.aicfoundation.com

Founded in 1983, the AIC Foundation opposes uncontrolled immigration into the United States, believing that it poses a grave threat to the rule of law in the country. The foundation indentifies illegal immigration as the greatest threat; however, the organization also advocates for increased governmental control to limit legal immigration. Books, pamphlets, and videos produced by the AIC Foundation can be accessed or purchased online.

Center for Immigration Studies (CIS)

1522 K Street NW, Suite 820, Washington, DC   20005-1202
(202) 466-8185 • fax: (202) 466-8076
e-mail: center@cis.org
Web site: www.cis.org

An independent think tank founded in 1985, CIS examines the ways that immigration affects the United States from economic, social, and demographic viewpoints. The center advocates for immigration policy that takes the national interest into account first, above all other factors. Additionally, CIS supports increased regulation to limit the number of immigrants admitted to the country so that those who are granted citizenship have a greater opportunity to succeed. CIS reports, testimony, and articles cover a variety of topics ranging from immigration history to costs of immigration, legal and illegal immigration to the impact on African Americans, and assimilation to guestworkers. All of these publications can be accessed on CIS's Web site.

Council on Foreign Relations (CFR)
The Harold Pratt House, 58 East 68th Street
New York, NY   10065
(212) 434-9400 • fax: (212) 434-9800
Web site: www.cfr.org

CFR provides educational information on important foreign policy issues facing the United States today. The council does not limit its audience to one specific group, seeking instead to inform everyone from government officials to scholars, journalists to educators, and civic and religious leaders to the average American citizen. CFR does not take official positions on any of the issues that it covers; however, reports and backgrounders published by the council cover many aspects of the immigration debate, and individual scholars to present their own viewpoints in their reports, which cover economic as well as societal and cultural issues. These publications are all available online; *Foreign Affairs* is the official journal of CFR.

Federation for American Immigration Reform (FAIR)
25 Massachusetts Ave. NW, Suite 330
Washington, DC   20001
(202) 328-7004 • fax: (202) 387-3447
Web site: www.fairus.org

FAIR is a membership organization open to all American citizens who are concerned with the current direction of immigration policy. The organization promotes immigration policy reform that ensures Americans in the present and the future have the opportunity to achieve happiness and success. FAIR worries that uncontrolled immigration has a negative effect on national security, jobs, health care, education, the environment, and the rule of law, and it encourages lawmakers to consider these effects carefully when deciding policy. FAIR's Web site offers e-ports and fact sheets on numerous immigration-related topics.

Heritage Foundation
214 Massachusetts Ave. NE, Washington, DC   20002
(202) 546-4400
e-mail: info@heritage.org
Web site: www.heritage.org

As a conservative public policy institute, Heritage seeks to promote the ideals of free enterprise, limited government, traditional American values, and a strong national defense. Heritage advocates for an immigration policy that welcomes immigrants who enter the United States through the proper legal channels and imposes restrictions to deter and punish those who enter illegally. Further, the organization believes that the U.S. border must be secure, but border policy must not be so stringent as to restrict commerce. Publications by foundation scholars addressing the issues of immigration can be read online.

John Birch Society
PO Box 8040, Appleton, WI   54912
(920) 749-3780
Web site: www.jbs.org

Founded in 1958, the John Birch Society is a conservative public policy organization that promotes the principles of personal freedom and limited government. The society works to ensure that no policies passed by the government infringe of the freedoms guaranteed American citizens by the Constitution. Illegal immigration is a great concern to the society, and it advocates for increased governmental restriction and enforcement to curb and control this problem. Reports on suggested legislation to address illegal immigration can be read on the organization's Web site.

National Council of La Raza (NCLR)
Raul Yzaguirre Building, 1126 16th Street NW
Washington, DC   20036
(202) 785-1670
Web site: www.nclr.org

NCLR has been working since 1968 to ensure that Hispanic Americans are afforded the same rights and opportunities as all other U.S. citizens. The council is actively involved in policy analysis and advocacy on many immigration-related issues such as the REAL ID Act, Comprehensive Immigration Reform, and the DREAM Act. Reports on these policies and others can be read on the NCLR Web site along with general immigration facts and policy briefs.

National Immigration Forum
50 F Street NW, Suite 300, Washington, DC   20001
(202) 347-0040 • fax: (202) 347-0058
Web site: www.immigrationforum.org

The National Immigration Forum was founded in 1982 as an immigrant rights organization with the goal of ensuring the all those who immigrate to the United States are granted their due rights. The forum seeks to achieve its mission, "To embrace and uphold America's tradition as a nation of immigrants," by reaching out to both policymakers and the American public and encouraging them to engage with the issues of immigration and support those who seek to establish their families and lives in the United States. Backgrounders, fact sheets, and issue papers can all be downloaded from the forum's Web site.

National Immigration Law Center (NILC)
3435 Wilshire Blvd., Suite 2850, Los Angeles, CA   90010
(213) 639-3900 • fax: (213) 639-3911
e-mail: info@nilc.org
Web site: www.nilc.org

NILC works to ensure that the rights of low-income immigrants and their families are protected. Specifically, the center focuses on employment laws and restriction of public services as imposed by the 1996 immigration reform laws. NILC works in many capacities, providing policy analysis, litigation, training and conferences, and publications such as the newsletter *Immigrants' Rights Update*, published eight times a year, and the electronic newsletter *E-mail Benefits Update*. Information about the organization's current projects and work can be found on the NILC Web site.

National Network for Immigrant and Refugee Rights (NNIRR)
310 8th Street, Suite 303, Oakland, CA   94607
(510) 465-1984 • fax: (510) 465-1885
e-mail: nnirr@nnirr.org
Web site: www.nnirr.org

NNIRR advocates for a national immigration and refugee policy that is just and ensures that the rights of all those coming to the United States are observed. To achieve these goals, the network coordinates efforts between local, national, and global groups seeking to improve the conditions of immigrants in the United States. Additionally, NNIRR seeks to educate all individuals about the hardships immigrants face as a result of current U.S. immigration policy. Reports and commentary on immigrant issues in the United States are available on the NNIRR Web site.

Negative Population Growth (NPG)
2861 Duke Street, Suite 36, Alexandria, VA   22314
(703) 370-9510 • (703) 370-9514
e-mail: npg@npg.org
Web site: www.npg.org

NPG believes that in the United States and globally the current levels of population growth are unsustainable are will have a detrimental effect on the world that is already beginning to be apparent. Among the solutions offered to halt population growth in the United States, NPG advocates for policy allows individuals to enter the country at the same rate that people leave it; so, if 200,000 people leave the country each year, then 200,000 people will be allowed to immigrate to the country. Reports on these and other issues are accessible on the NPG Web site.

U.S. Citizenship and Immigration Services (USCIS)
Department of Homeland Security, Washington, DC   20528
(202) 282-8000
Web site: www.uscis.gov

USCIS is the branch of the U.S. Department of Homeland Security in charge of immigration to the United States. Immigration services, policies, and priorities all originate from the USCIS. Additionally, this government agency also makes decisions regarding who will be allowed to lawfully enter the United States and with what designation, for example with an immigrant visa or as a refugee. The USCIS Web site provides additional information about the services it provides as well as current immigration laws and regulation.

Bibliography of Books

Edward H. Alden   *The Closing of the American Border: Terrorism, Immigration, and Security Since 9/11*. New York: Harper, 2008.

George J. Borjas, ed.   *Mexican Immigration to the United States*. Chicago: University of Chicago Press, 2007.

Aviva Chomsky   *"They Take Our Jobs!": And 20 Other Myths About Immigration*. Boston, MA: Beacon, 2007.

Deepa Fernandes   *Targeted: Homeland Security and the Business of Immigration*. New York: Seven Stories, 2007.

Jane Guskin and David L. Wilson   *The Politics of Immigration: Questions and Answers*. New York: Monthly Review, 2007.

J.D. Hayworth with Joseph J. Eule   *Whatever It Takes: Illegal Immigration, Border Security, and the War on Terror*. Washington, DC: Regenery, 2006.

Paul W. Hickman and Thomas P. Curtis, eds.   *Immigration Crisis: Issues, Policies and Consequences*. New York: Nova Science, 2008.

Earl Ofari Hutchinson   *The Latino Challenge to Black America*. Los Angeles: Middle Passage, 2007.

Robin Dale Jacobson — *The New Nativism: Proposition 187 and the Debate Over Immigration.* Minneapolis, MN: University of Minnesota Press, 2008.

Kevin R. Johnson — *Opening the Floodgates: Why America Needs to Rethink Its Border and Immigration Laws.* New York: New York University Press, 2007.

Richard C. Jones, ed. — *Immigrants Outside Megalopolis: Ethnic Transformation in the Heartland.* Lanham, MD: Lexington, 2008.

Mark Krikorian — *The New Case Against Immigration: Both Legal and Illegal.* New York: Sentinel, 2008.

Jennifer E. Lansford, Kirby Deater-Deckard, and Marc H. Bornstein, eds. — *Immigrant Families in Contemporary Society.* New York: Guilford, 2007.

Michael C. LeMay — *Illegal Immigration: A Reference Handbook.* Santa Barbara, CA: ABC-CLIO, 2007.

Heather Mac Donald, Victor Davis Hanson, and Steven Malanga — *The Immigration Solution: A Better Plan than Today's.* Chicago: Ivan R. Dee, 2007.

Douglas S. Massey, ed. — *New Faces in New Places: The Changing Geography of American Immigration.* New York: Russell Sage Foundation, 2008.

Dowell Myers — *Immigrants and Boomers: Forging a New Social Contract for the Future of America.* New York: Russell Sage Foundation, 2007.

Lina Newton — *Illegal, Alien, or Immigrant: The Politics of Immigration Reform.* New York: New York University Press, 2008.

Margaret Sands Orcho — *Immigration and the American Dream: Battling the Political Hype and Hysteria.* Lanham, MD: Rowman & Littlefield, 2008.

John Powell — *Immigration.* New York: Facts on File, 2007.

Fernando Romero — *Hyperborder: The Contemporary U.S.-Mexico Border and Its Future.* New York: Princeton Architectural Press, 2008.

Rachel Rubin and Jeffrey Melnick — *Immigration and American Popular Culture: An Introduction.* New York: New York University Press, 2007.

Rinku Sen, with Fekkak Mamdouh — *The Accidental American: Immigration and Citizenship in the Age of Globalization.* San Francisco: Berrett-Koehler, 2008.

Mary C. Waters and Reed Ueda, with Helen B. Marrow — *The New Americans: A Guide to Immigration Since 1965.* Cambridge, MA: Harvard University Press, 2007.

Russell O. Wright — *Chronology of Immigration in the United States.* Jefferson, NC: McFarland & Co., 2008.

Index

A

Abouhalima, Mahmed, 159, 160
Abouhalima, Mohammed, 159
Abu Mezer, Gazi Ibrahim, 151
Acculturation, 87, 92–93
Ackers, Becky, 22–29
Adams, Margaret, 85–95
Afghanistan, 160, 204, 206
African Americans
    Asian business owners and, 43
    economic effect of immigra-
        tion on, 36–44
    education and, 42
    Hispanic business owners and,
        43
    intimidation by illegal aliens,
        34
    low-rent housing, 42
    negative stereotypes, 43
    perception of immigrants, 41
    recession and, 42
    as residual labor pool, 39
    unions and, 39
    urban labor markets and, 40
    war and, 39
Al-Midhar, Khalid, 154–155
Al Qaeda
    domestic warfare and, 149
    flying lessons, 210
    illegal aliens and, 150, 157,
        158
    immigration policies and, 151,
        154, 160
    overstayers and, 158, 187
    recruitment, 168
    Visa Waiver Program (WVP)
        and, 167–168

Al-Qahtani, Mohamed, 152, 156
Alabama, 71
Alaska, 71, 139
Alexander, Lamar, 65
Alfred, King, 143
Algebra, 79
American Association of Motor
    Vehicles Administrators
    (AAMVA), 131
American Elections Act, 62
American Policy Center, 122
Amnesty
    anti-amnesty sentiment, 15,
        16, 124, 142
    Bush amnesty program, 148
    college students and, 142
    immigration control and, 161
    legislation, 172
    political parties and, 16, 66
    terrorists and, 152, 160
Anchor babies, 142
Anti-immigration movement, 48
Argentina, 179, 180
Arizona
    border fence and, 104, 106
    English language law, 71
    non-English speaking students
        and education, 76, 79–80,
        82, 91
    sheltered English immersion
        and, 79–80, 82
Arkansas, 47, 71
Arrest, 157
Asian business owners, 43
Asylum, 150
Atta, Mohammed, 151, 154, 158
Australia, 175, 180

Ayn Rand Institute, 132
Aztlan movement, 34

B

Baca, Joe, 65
Balkanization, 34
Bank accounts, 157, 159, 193
Basic Pilot, 118, 124
Battle of Edington, 143
Bearers of Global Jihad?: Immigration and National Security After 9/11 (Nixon Center), 168
Belarus, 142
Bell, Alexander Graham, 140
Benhali bilingual programs, 78–79
Berlin Wall, 180
Bigotry, 69–73
Bilingual education
    Chinese bilingual education programs, 77–78, 83
    families and, 93
    as financial burden, 53
    ineffectiveness of, 76–77
    monolingual teachers and, 95
    Spanish bilingual education programs, 78, 79
    as taught in English, 77–78
    teacher training and, 93–94
    transitional bilingual education, 75, 86, 88–89
See also Language; Non-English speaking students
Bilingual maintenance, 76
Bilingual voting ballots, 62
Binalshibh, Ramzi, 152
Binswanger, Harry, 132–140
Biometric Visa Program, 154
Blackwell, Kenneth, 64–68
Border communities, 59
Border Crossing Card, 106

Border fence
    Constitutional law and, 110–111
    criticism of, 105–111
    as deterrent to illegal immigration, 100–104, 103, 131
    as environmentally damaging, 109–110
    legislation, 15–16, 101, 104, 109, 123
    See also Border protection; Mexico
Border Patrol, 108, 154, 156
Border protection
    cost effectiveness of, 198–199
    enforcement only approach, 201
    globalization and, 25, 27
    intelligence and, 196
    irrelevance of, 27
    legislation, 15–16, 101, 104, 109
    Minuteman Project, 98–99
    political inaction and, 207–208
    Roman Empire and, 31
    terrorism and, 196–200, 204–209
See also Border fence
Bosnia, 142
Boston University, 74
Boudreaux, Donald J., 22–29
Brazil, 164
Brookings Institution, 107
Brunei, 175
Buckeye Institute, 64
Bureau of Consular Affairs (U.S. Dept. of State), 150, 153
Bureau of Customs and Border Protection (DHS), 154
Burmese refugees, 35
Burundi, 142

Bush, George W.
Address on Immigration Reform, 14, 15
amnesty for illegal aliens, 148
border security and, 101, 103, 106
on first war of 21st century, 149
guest worker program, 148, 205
Hispanic voters and, 17
immigration reform and, 98, 110, 200
language abilities, 72–73
mortgage crisis and, 32
Visa Waiver Program (VWP) and, 175–176, 180

C

California, 24, 31, 39, 51, 52, 65, 71
border fence and, 102–104, 106
immigration policies, 145
Minuteman Project, 98–99
non-English speaking students and education, 76, 79–84, 86, 91, 93
Proposition 227, 80, 83
Camarota, Steven A., 20–21, 50–54
Canada, 67, 156, 175, 199
Capital, 25
Capital punishment, 206
Capone, Al, 160
Carnegie, Andrew, 140
Castro, Fidel, 27
CATO Institute, 126, 130, 175
CBS News, 16–17
Center for Comparative Immigration Studies, 106–107, 205

Center for Immigration Studies, 20, 36, 51, 110, 147, 150, 168, 183, 189
Center for Trade Policy Studies, 175
Charities, 27
Chertoff, Michael, 106, 109–110, 124
Chinese bilingual education programs, 77–78, 83
Chinese Exclusion Act, 24
Chinese immigrants, 24, 35
ChoicePoint, 199
Christian Science Monitor (newspaper), 16
CIA, 154, 159
Civil Rights Act Title VI, 90
Clinton, Bill, 103, 139
Clinton, Hilary, 68, 129
CNN, 68
Colorado, 17, 56, 71
Columbia University, 43
Compliance Enforcement Unit (CEU), 185
Congressional Black Caucus Foundation, 36
Congressional Budget Office, 109
Congressional Research Service, 109, 179
Convicts, 24
Cornelius, Wayne, 106–107, 109, 205
Cortes, Patricia, 26
Cox, Stephen, 144
"Coyotes", 107
Crime
deportation and, 123
economic costs of, 30
immigration policies and, 135

Mexico's extradition policy, 206

motor vehicle crimes, 33–34

murder, 33, 183, 191, 206–207

organized crime, 35, 188, 190–191

prison overcrowding and, 34

San Diego border fence and, 103

sanctuary policies and, 33

See also Terrorism

Cuba, 27

Czech Republic, 176–180, 188, 191, 192

D

Dalmia, Shikha, 55–59

Data Management Improvement Act of 2000, 184

Day labor positions, 40

Declaration of Independence, 133

Defenders of Wildlife, 110

Democratic party

amnesty and, 16, 66

immigration reform and, 14–18

lawsuits over language requirements and, 65

public services for illegal aliens and, 57

Department of Motor Vehicles, 200

Departure tracking, 156

Deportation, 57, 58, 123, 142

deportation hearings, 151

enforcement of immigration laws, 157, 158

DeWeese, Tom, 122–131

Disease *See also* Medical care, 24

Doherty, Carrol, 41

DREAM (Development, Relief and Education for Alien Minors) Act, 142

Driver's licenses, 129, 157, 159, 170, 193, 197, 199

Driving habits, 33–34

Drug trafficking, 33–34, 100, 101, 103, 190–191

Dual citizenship, 211–212

E

E-passports, 210

Economy

capital, 25

cost of goods and services, 26

costs of education of illegal aliens, 15, 31–32, 56

economic costs of illegal alien crimes, 30

free market economics, 55

free trade, 25

illegal immigration as harmful to, 30–35

immigration as economically beneficial, 22–29

investors, 25

mortgage crisis, 30–32

open immigration and, 138–140

overstayer costs to taxpayers, 183

profits, 25

specialization in workforce, 24–25

Visa Waiver Program (VWP), and, 174–181

See also Employment; Wages

Education

African Americans and, 42

as available to illegal aliens, 56

costs of educating illegal
aliens, 15, 31–32, 53
economic success and, 53–54
low-skilled jobs and, 20
poverty and, 52
social service usage and, 54
wage levels and, 20, 37, 144
See also Bilingual education;
Schools
Egypt, 154, 206
El Salvador, 142
Elections. See Voting; Republican
party; Democratic party
Electronic Travel Authorization
(ETA), 180, 186
Emergency medical care, 56, 58
Employers, 114, 125, 208
Employment
African Americans and, 37–44
as chokepoint for immigration control, 159
day labor positions, 40
economic downturn and, 108
education and, 20
employment rates, 45–49
employment verification, 112–
131
English fluency and, 66–67
illegal aliens as "cheap" labor,
20, 34, 52, 110, 193, 208
industries employing illegal
aliens, 121
job displacement by illegal
aliens, 20, 26
lawsuits, 65
"off-the-books" employment
of illegal aliens, 116, 121
"on-the-books" employment
of illegal aliens, 15, 54, 56,
114–115, 121

population density and, 139–
140
right to employment, 133–134
termination of, 125
unemployment, 108, 138
wages, 20, 24–25, 34, 138
See also Wages
England, 139
English as official language of
United States, 64–68
English as second language. See
Non-English speaking students
English language learners (ELL)
See also Non-English speaking
students
Enhanced Border Security, 210
Environmental damage, 109–110
Equal Employment Opportunity
Commission (EEOC), 65
Estonia, 175, 188, 191, 192
European Union (EU), 177, 191–
192

F

Facial recognition software, 130
Family Research Council, 64
FBI, 65, 160, 185
Federation for American Immigra-
tion Reform (FAIR), 166, 167
Feeding programs in schools, 53
Fingerprinting, 154, 157, 164, 186
Florida, 39, 71, 158, 159
Food stamps, 56
Founding Fathers, 23
"Fourth-Generation" warfare, 149
France, 142–143, 169, 178, 211
Free labor markets, 25
Free market economics, 55

Free trade, 25
Fund, John, 65

G

Gambling, 191
Gangs, 34
GAO (Government Accountability Office), 188
Garver, Lloyd, 69–73
George Mason University, 22
Georgia, 57, 58, 71
Germany, 142–143, 178, 211
Gilchrest, Jim, 98–99
Gillchrest, Robert, 81
Gonzalez, Elian, 27
Gorbachev, Mikhail, 180
Government Accountability Office (GAO), 188
Greece, 178, 188, 190, 191
Green cards, 115, 116, 152, 191, 211
Gregory, Anthony, 136
Griswold, Daniel, 174–181
Guatemala, 142
Guest worker program, 25, 59, 161, 185, 205

H

Hamilton, Alexander, 140
Harper, Jim, 126, 130
Havel, Vaclav, 180
Hawaii, 71, 139, 191
Health care. *See* Medical care
Health insurance, 52
Heller, Dean, 62–63
Heritage Foundation, 112
Hinojosa, Juan, 98–99

Hispanic population, 16–17, 43, 110, 148
  See also Mexico
Hmong people, 35
Home front, 148–149
Housing, 42, 56
Human trafficking, 192
Hungary, 177, 178, 188, 189, 190, 191
Hunter, Duncan, 100–104
Hutchinson, Asa, 153

I

I-9 form, 115, 116
ICE. *See* Immigration and Customs Enforcement (ICE)
Idaho, 71
Identity theft and fraud, 115–116, 128
Illegal aliens
  apprehension of illegal aliens 1992–2004, 102
  arrest of, 123
  assimilation, 34
  bank accounts and, 157, 159
  crime and, 30, 33–35, 103, 123
  deportation and, 57, 58, 123, 142
  driver's licenses and, 157, 159–160
  as economically beneficial, 22–29
  as economically harmful, 30–35
  guest-worker programs, 25, 59
  job displacement of U.S. citizens and, 20, 26
  mortgage crisis and, 30–32

as motor vehicle drivers, 33–34
population growth, 14–15
prison inmates, 30, 34
social service usage, 15
taxes and, 15, 54, 56
as taxpayer burden, 21, 57
wages and, 20, 24–25
See also Bilingual education; Crime; Education; Employment; Immigration; Overstayers; Social services; Taxes; Terrorism
Illinois, 71
Immigration
    acculturation and, 87, 92–93
    anti-immigration movement, 48
    assimilation, 34
    crime and, 35
    distribution of immigrants, 39
    as economically beneficial, 22–29
    education levels and, 50, 52
    employment as reason for, 39
    employment rates and, 45–49
    guest-worker programs, 25, 59, 161, 185
    historic limitations on, 24
    immigration reform, 14–18, 98, 101, 110, 166, 167, 172, 198–199
    open immigration, 132–146
    as outside federal jurisdiction, 23–24
    sanctuary policies, 158–160
    social services exploitation and, 50–54
    unconstitutional immigration laws, 28–29
See also Illegal aliens; Overstayers; Visa

Immigration and Customs Enforcement (ICE), 183, 185, 192
Immigration Reform and Control Act (IRCA), 124, 172
India, 142
Indiana, 71
Indonesia, 154
Inquiry Into the Nature and Causes of the Wealth of Nations (Smith), 24
Insanity, 24
Internal Revenue Service (IRS), 57, 127
International Civil Aviation Organizations (ICAO), 131
Investors, 25
Iowa, 71
Iran, 103, 142, 206
Iraq, 149, 204, 207
Ireland, 190
Islam
    "home front" war and, 149
    terrorists threats and, 149, 152, 167–168, 204, 206
    Visa Waiver Program (WVP) and, 167–168, 175, 177–178, 211
See also Terrorism
Ismoil, Eyad, 159

J

Jaguars, 109
Japan, 175
Jarrah, Ziad Samir, 158
Jimmerson, Jo Beth, 92
John Birch Society, 30
Johnson, Randel, 17
Jones, Kellie M., 85–95

Jones, Walter B., 62
Judis, John B., 48

K

Kansas, 71
Kansi, Mir Aimal, 159
Kennedy, Ted, 17
Kentucky, 71
Know-Nothings, 48
Kochhar, Rakesh, 45–49
Krikorian, Mark, 110, 147–161, 187

L

Language
    bigotry and, 69–73
    bilingual voting ballots, 62
    costs of multilingual population, 67
    education and, 53, 70
    employment lawsuits over, 65
    English as official language of United States, 64–68
    public opinion, 65–66
    See also Bilingual education
Las Vegas Review-Journal (newspaper), 141
Las Vegas Sun (newspaper), 62
Latvia, 188, 189, 190, 191
Lebanon, 103, 206
Legal permanent resident (LPR), 211
Legislation
    American Elections Act, 62
    Civil Rights Act Title VI, 90
    Data Management Improvement Act of 2000, 184
    DREAM (Development, Relief and Education for Alien Minors) Act, 142
    Immigration Reform and Control Act (IRCA), 124, 172
    Personal Responsibility and Work Opportunity and Reconciliation Act (PRWORA), 139
    Real ID Act, 25
    Secure Borders, Economic Opportunity and Immigration Reform Act, 15, 101, 104, 109
    unconstitutional immigration laws, 28–29
    Visa Reform Act of 2002, 210
    Visa Waiver Permanent Program Act, 184
    Voting Rights Act, 62
Leiken, Robert S., 168
Lewis, Ethan, 26
Libertarians, 143–145, 175
Liptak, Adam, 110
Lithuania, 188, 189, 190, 191
Los Angeles International Airport, 152
Los Angeles Unified School District, 81
Louisiana, 71
Low-rent housing, 42
Low-skilled jobs, education levels and, 20
Lunatics, 24

M

Mac Donald, Heather, 33
Mainstreaming non-English speaking students, 74, 82, 85, 89–90

Malanga, Steven, 20–21
Malkin, Michelle, 32
Malta, 188
Manhattan Institute, 20
March, David, 206
Martinez, Gebe, 17
Maryland, 118, 158
Mason, Melanie, 105–111
Massachusetts
    English language law, 71
    Massachusetts General Laws
        Chapter 71A, 89, 93
    non-English speaking students
        and education, 76
    Question 2, 86, 88, 90, 91, 93,
        94
    sheltered English immersion
        teaching and, 79–80, 82
Massachusetts Comprehensive As-
    sessment System (MCAS), 91
Massachusetts Department of
    Education, 87, 90, 91, 94
Massey, Douglas, 107
Mathematics, 79, 80
McCain, John, 16, 129
Medi-Cal, 52
Medicaid, 52, 56, 57
Medical care
    deportation fears and, 58
    emergency medical care, 56,
        58
    health insurance, 52
    illegal aliens and, 15, 31, 52,
        56
    Kennedy and, 17
    statistics on, 52
Medicare, 55, 56
Meskini, Abdelghani, 156, 159
Mexico
    Aztlan movement, 34

    illegal immigration and, 20,
        107, 142, 172, 205–206
    immigrant labor and, 20
    North American Perimeter
        Safety Zone, 199
    terrorist access to U.S. and,
        101, 104, 204–206
Mezer, Abu, 156
Mill, John Stuart, 11
Millennium Plot, 156, 159
Minnesota, 210
Minuteman Project, 98–99, 208
Mission creep, 131–132
Mississippi, 25, 71
Missouri, 71
Mocny, Robert, 165
Money laundering, 191
Money transfers, 159
Monolingual teachers, 95
Montana, 71
Morgan State University, 36
Morocco, 154
Morris, Frank, 36–44
Mortgage crisis, 30–32
Moussaoui, Zacharias, 168, 169,
    210
Mowbray, Joe, 151
Mujica, Mauro E., 67
Muñoz, Cecilia, 110
Murder, 33, 183, 191, 206–207
Mutual Assured Destruction, 153

N

NAFTA (North American Free
    Trade Agreement), 32–33
National Council of La Raza, 110,
    148
National Guard, 208
National identification card, 130

National Immigration Forum, 16

National Research Council, 59

National Strategy for Homeland Security, 150

NATO, 177

Nebraska, 71

Nevada, 47, 62, 145

New Hampshire, 71

New Jersey, 139, 159

New Mexico, 104

New York, 25, 78

New York subway bombing, 187

New York Times (newspaper), 110

New Zealand, 175

9/11 Commission, 155

9/11 terrorist attack
   al Qaeda recruitment and, 168
   border protection and, 204
   FBI response, 160
   illegal aliens and, 151, 210
   intelligence collection and, 200
   overstayers and, 183
   US-VISIT and, 164, 175
   visa requirements and, 154, 170, 187, 189

Ninth Amendment, 27

Nixon Center, 168

Non-English speaking students
   acculturation and, 87, 92–93
   Benhali bilingual programs, 78–79
   bilingual maintenance, 76
   Chinese bilingual education programs, 77–78, 83
   dropout rates for, 90
   English immersion and, 74
   English-only mandates, 91
   ESL pullout, 75
   family involvement and, 93
   mainstreaming non-English speaking students, 74, 82, 85, 89–90
   monolingual teachers and, 95
   sheltered/structured English immersion, 75, 78–84, 85, 87
   sink-or-swim mainstream approach, 75, 85, 88–89
   Spanish bilingual education programs, 78, 79
   standardized test scores, 80–82, 91
   teacher training and, 93–94
   transitional bilingual education, 75–78, 86, 88–89
   two-way bilingual education, 75–76
   types of teaching for, 75–76
   See also Bilingual education

Noorani, Ali, 16

North American Perimeter Safety Zone, 199

North Carolina, 71

North Dakota, 71

Norwood, Charlie, 57

NSEERS (National Security Entry-Exit Registration System), 185

Nuclear threats, 152–153

O

Obama, Barack
   English as official language of U.S. and, 68
   fast-tracking immigrant legal status, 16
   passport, 129
   Statement on Immigration Reform, 14

"Off-the-books" employment of illegal aliens, 116, 121

Office of Immigration Statistics, 14

Oklahoma, 58

"On-the-books" employment of illegal aliens, 15, 54, 56, 114–116, 121

Open immigration, 132–146

Operation Community Shield, 183

Organization of Economic Cooperation and Development, 178

Overstayers
al Qaeda and, 158, 187
definition of, 106
dysfuntional immigration system and, 197
employment and, 113, 193
FBI tracking, 185–186
illegal alien population and, 183
profile of, 151–152
as security threat, 182–193
terrorism and, 154, 158, 160, 182, 183, 202
US-VISIT and, 199
visa exit controls and, 156, 184, 185, 187
Visa Waiver Program (VWP) and, 178

P

Pakistan, 154, 206

Parti Québécois, 67

Passenger manifests, 157, 185

Passports
E-verify and, 124
lost/stolen passports, 191
machine-readable passports, 176
privacy issues, 129
rules for obtaining, 126–127

US-VISIT and, 156–157, 164, 184
Visa Waiver Program (VWP) and, 166

Paupers, 24

Pelosi, Nancy, 65

Personal Responsibility and Work Opportunity and Reconciliation Act (PRWORA), 139

Pew Hispanic Center, 45, 46, 106, 205

Pew Research Center, 41

Photographs
biometric information in passports, 130, 154, 156, 164, 186, 210
employment verification and, 124

Poland, 177, 178

Politico.com, 17

Polygamists, 24

Population density, 139–140

Populist party, 48

Portugal, 176–177, 179

Poverty, 52, 54, 57

Princeton University, 107

Prison inmates population, 30, 34

Project Pinpoint, 186

Property taxes, 59

Prostitution, 24, 191, 192

R

Racism, 99

Rand, Ayn, 137, 140

Reading, 80

Reagan, Ronald, 180

Real ID Act, 25, 196, 199–200

Reason, 137

Reason Foundation, 55

Rector, Robert E., 112–121
Reid, Richard, 168, 169, 210
Report on the Legalized Alien Population, 172
Republican party
    immigration reform and, 14–17
    lawsuits over language requirements and, 65
    public services for illegal aliens and, 57
Ressam, Ahmed, 152, 156
RFID microchips, 130
Rights, 133–137
Roman Empire, 31
Rossell, Christine, 74–84
"Run letters", 158
Russia, 190
Russian immigrants, 35
Ryan, Mary, 150

S

Sabal Palm Audubon Center, 109
Salameh, Mohammed, 151–152, 159
Sales taxes, 55, 59
Salvation Army, 65
Sanctuary policies, 158–160
Saudi Arabia, 154, 156, 206
Schools
    African Americans and, 42
    bilingual education, 53, 70
    costs of education of illegal aliens, 15, 31–32, 56
    feeding programs in schools, 53
    statistics of immigrants in, 52
See also Education

Secure Borders, Economic Opportunity and Immigration Reform Act, 15–16, 101, 104, 109
Semion Mogilevich Organization, 190
Senate Judiciary Subcommittee on Immigration, 17
SEVIS (Student and Exchange Visitor Information System), 185
Sheltered/structured English immersion, 75, 78–84, 85, 86
"Shoe bomber", 210
Sierra Club, 110
Sikorsky, Igor, 140
Simcox, Chris, 98
Singapore, 175
Singer, Audrey, 107–109
Sink-or-swim mainstream approach for non-English speaking students, 75, 85, 88–89
Slovakia, 177, 178, 188, 189, 190, 191
Smith, Adam, 24
Smuggling, 101, 103, 107, 191
Social Security Administration
    database, 125–126
    "earnings suspense file," 59
    employment of illegal aliens and, 34, 55, 56, 57, 59
    employment verification and, 114–120, 124, 126–128
    mission creep and, 130
Social services
    education levels and, 54
    illegal alien use of, 55–59, 57
    immigrant exploitation of, 50–54
    legislation, 139
    taxpayer burden and, 21
Socialism, 32

Solntsevskaya Organization, 190–191
Somalia, 206
South Carolina, 71
South Dakota, 71
South Korea, 177, 178, 188, 191, 192
Spain, 206, 211
Spanish bilingual education programs, 78, 79
Specialization in workforce, 24–25
SportsLine.com, 69
Standardized test scores, 80–82, 91
Steinlight, Stephen M., 167–168
Stock, Margaret D., 194–202
Stowaways on ships, 156
Sudan, 206
Suicide attacks, 149, 151
Supreme Court, 24
Suprynowicz, Vin, 141–146
Syria, 103, 206

T

Tancredo, Tom, 17, 56
Tasmania, 142
Tax evasion, 160
Taxes
    illegal aliens as taxpayer burden, 21, 31–32
    illegal aliens as taxpayers, 54, 56, 57
    property taxes, 59
    sales taxes, 55, 59
    social services for illegal aliens and, 21
    See also Social Security Administration
Teacher training, 93–94
Temple University, 203

Tennessee, 65, 71
Tenth Amendment, 27
Terrorism
    border fence and, 101
    identification of terrorists, 169
    immigration policies and, 147–161
    London bombings, 204
    overstayers and, 154, 160, 182, 183
    US-VISIT and, 164, 175
    visas requirements and, 150, 154, 157, 167, 169, 170
    See also Islam; 9/11 terrorist attack
Test scores, 80–82
Texas, 39, 98–99, 104, 109
Thailand, 142
Thompson, Art, 30–35
Ting, Jan C., 203–212
Tizegha, Abdel Hakim, 156
Tourism industry, 170, 175, 176, 211
Transitional bilingual education, 75, 86, 88–89
Transportation Security Administration (TSA), 129–130
Two-way bilingual education, 75–76

U

Unemployment, 108, 138
Unions, 39
United Arab Emirates, 154
United Kingdom, 169, 172, 178, 211
United Nations Human Rights Commission, 66
University of California at San Diego, 107, 205

Unskilled workers, 37
Unz, Ron, 86, 94–95
Urban Institute, 57
Urban, Nancy, 20
Uruguay, 179, 180
U.S. Army Reserves, 208
U.S. Border Patrol, 27
U.S. Census Bureau, 14, 50
U.S. Chamber of Commerce, 17
U.S. Congress, 28, 194, 195, 210, 212
U.S. Constitution, 27, 110–111
U.S. Department of Commerce, 176
U.S. Department of Education, 94, 127
U.S. Department of Health and Human Services, 127
U.S. Department of Homeland Security
    border fence and, 101, 104, 106, 109–110
    Bureau of Customs and Border Protection, 154
    employment verification and, 114, 117, 118, 123
    illegal alien population estimates, 14
    immigrant screening and, 169
    immigration control and, 149
    overstayers and, 184
    transfer of information from, 131
    US-VISIT and, 164, 185
    Visa Waiver Program (VWP), 180
U.S. Department of Justice, 65
U.S. Department of State
    dual citizenship and, 212
    as issuer of visas, 153–154, 170
    overstayers and, 187
    religious freedom survey, 177–178
    Visa Waiver Program (VWP) and, 179, 188, 209
    visas and terrorists, 150–151
U.S. history, 79
U.S. House of Representatives, 28, 194, 210
U.S. Military Academy, 194
U.S. Senate, 142
U.S. Supreme Court, 212
US-VISIT (United States Visitor and Immigrant Status Indicator Technology), 156–157, 164, 184–185, 196, 199
USA Patriot Act, 210
USCIS (United States Citizen and Immigration Service), 119–120
U.S.S. *Cole*, 154
Utah, 71

V

Vaughan, Jessica M., 182–193
Virginia, 71, 130, 159
Virtual border, 165
Visa
    Biometric Visa Program, 154
    criminals obtaining, 183
    E-verify and, 124
    ease of obtaining, 155
    entry-exit records, 156, 184, 185, 187
    legislation, 104, 109, 184, 210
    terrorists and, 150, 154, 157, 167, 169
    US-VISIT and, 156–157
    visa fraud, 188, 191
    visa requirements, 209
See also Overstayers

Visa Reform Act of 2002, 210
Visa Waiver Permanent Program
    Act, 184
Visa Waiver Program (VWP)
    argument for expansion of,
        174–181
    country qualification for, 176–
        180, 184, 189–191
    Electronic Travel Authoriza-
        tion (ETA) process, 186
    overstayers and, 178
    as security threat, 166–173
    terrorism and, 169, 170
    tourism industry and, 170
Visigoths, 31
Voting
    bilingual voting ballots, 62, 70
    Hispanic population voting
        trends, 16–17
Voting Rights Act, 62

W

W-2 form, 116
W-4 form, 116
Wages
    education and, 20, 37, 144
    immigrant effect on, 24–25,
        34
    labor pool and, 138
    unskilled workers and, 37
    See also Economy; Employment
Wahabbi doctrine, 168
Wall Street, 48
Wall Street Journal (newspaper),
    42, 65
War, 39
War on Terror, 195
Washington, Booker T., 38
Washington Post (newspaper), 164
Washington Times (newspaper), 15
Watch lists, 154, 156
Welfare system. *See* Social services
Westat, 118
Wolfowitz, Paul, 149
World Trade Center bombing,
    151–152, 159, 184, 187, 210
Wyoming, 71

Y

Yemen, 103, 206